TOWER Air
FRYER COOKBOOK FOR
BEGINNERS UK

1500 days of affordable and delicious Tower Air Fryer Recipes for You And Your Family,

Using European Units of Measurement

GLADYS W. URIBE

Table of Contents

Introduction

UK Tower Air Fryers are versatile and convenient kitchen appliances that will work for any kitchen. They can be used for preparing all types of dishes. With an air fryer at hand, your imagination is the only limitation to what savory meals you can enjoy. If you are still debating whether to get one, below are some reasons that might convince you to take the plunge.

Chapter 1
Reasons for Using A Tower Air Fryer

FROZEN FOODS TASTE BETTER

Frozen foods are cheap and easy to prepare. They ensure you can avoid the hassle of sourcing fresh ingredients. However, the downside is that you have to tradeoff flavorful meals for convenience.

With an air fryer, that can be different. The UK Tower Air Fryers use vortex technology that unlocks flavors deep within the blandest frozen meals. It helps to improve not only the test but the texture as well. You can enjoy noticeably better meals, even when you only have time to cook frozen food.

REFRESH YOUR TAKEOUT

When you order takeout, the 30 minutes it takes to arrive at your doorstep can ruin it. Since it is wrapped tightly for safe delivery, the hot air inside often ruins the texture and taste. You can refresh it by sticking it in the air fryer for five minutes, returning it to a crispy consistency.

REHEAT LAST NIGHT'S LEFTOVERS

Most people often stick leftovers in the microwave and they do not taste nice. In most cases, the food comes out soggy, with some having cold spots. An air fryer does not suffer from such shortcomings. The circulating hot air ensures leftovers are evenly heated to a crispy consistency.

It especially shines when it comes to reheating pizza. You never have to worry about soggy pizza with cold spots ever again. Everything comes out tasting, feeling, and smelling fresh as if you just took it out of the pizza oven.

THEY ARE CHEAP TO OPERATE

Energy and food prices have been reaching all-time highs, which has caused many families to tighten their budgets. However, that should not mean eating bad food. An air fryer will reduce how much energy you use for cooking food, leading to better meals and recipes. Everyone will have a wide grin during meal times with an air fryer. Running an air fryer can cost as little as $.20 per meal.

ENJOY HEALTHIER MEALS

If you love enjoying crispier meals, such as crispy French fries and chicken, the main alternative is deep-frying. However, deep-frying is not healthy at all. Doctors recommend that people reduce the deep-fried foods they consume.

When you use an air fryer, you only need a teaspoon of oil. You do not have to worry about risking your health when you enjoy your favorite fried delights. An air fryer also reduces the fat in your food. For instance, when you cook chicken wings in the air fryer, some fat drains off, which is good for you.

COOK FASTER

Many people love cooking, but they do not have the time. You can cook most meals in 30 minutes or less with an air fryer. For instance, cooking fries will only take you 15 minutes at most. Some other meals, like fish cakes, will take 25 minutes or less.

CLEARING IS EASY

Unlike many other kitchen appliances, cleaning an air fryer is relatively easy. Modern air fryers are dishwasher safe, making cleaning even more manageable. Since they do not use up a lot of oil, you do not need to use any specialized techniques during cleaning.

INVESTING IN A QUALITY AIR FRYER IS EASY

Today, there are numerous models of UK Tower Air fryers. All of these air fryers come in various sizing and capabilities. For instance, some advanced models will let you cook a whole rotisserie chicken there. No matter the model you pick, the cost is $100 or less, with a few costing around $200. For a beginner, you can find models that cost as little as $50. You can avoid breaking the bank to enjoy some tasty meals.

GREAT FOR DECLUTTERING YOUR KITCHEN SPACE

An air fryer is an excellent option if you are trying to get rid of clutter. It is especially significant in a studio apartment with limited space. The air fryer is for you if you want to keep your kitchen countertop clear while also enjoying great meals.

NUMEROUS OPTIONS

One of the best things is that the air fryer can be configured for different purposes. There are general air fryers for simple use cases, or you can opt for complex ones that come with the latest gizmos. Modern air fryers come in different sizes, which means you can find one to prepare small meals for yourself or a big one to prepare meals for a medium-sized family.

Air fryers also come at numerous price points. It ensures you can test the waters with a cheap option before opting for a more advanced model as your needs increase. You can even purchase two or more to prepare your family's meals exclusively using air fryers. There is no limit to the options available.

THEY KEEP GETTING BETTER

Air fryers are continually upgraded. For instance, UK Tower Air Fryers are always coming out with new advanced features to increase ease and convenience for everyone. You will be better prepared to pick advanced models by getting in right now. In the future, air fryers could come with enough features to replace almost every cooking appliance in your kitchen.

ENJOY DIVERSE RECIPES

You can enjoy thousands of recipes with an air fryer. As technology advances, so do the possibilities. You can handle running out of recipes to prepare. In this cookbook, you will find fabulous, tantalizing recipes you can prepare with ingredients in your local store.

There is something for you to enjoy in every season. You can also play around with the ingredients to come up with unique creations. While you may not perfect your cooking the first time you use it, the quality will improve as you get used to it.

Get an air fryer and try some of these great recipes!

Chapter 2
Breakfasts

Oat Porridge with Chia Seeds
Prep time: 10 minutes | Cook time: 5 minutes | Serves 4

- 2 tablespoons peanut butter
- 4 tablespoons honey
- 1 tablespoon butter, melted
- 4 cups milk
- 2 cups oats
- 1 cup chia seeds

1. Preheat the air fryer to 200°C.
2. Put the peanut butter, honey, butter, and milk in a bowl and stir to mix. Add the oats and chia seeds and stir.
3. Transfer the mixture to a bowl and bake in the air fryer for 5 minutes. Give another stir before serving.

Halloumi Pepper and Spinach Omelet
Prep time: 10 minutes | Cook time: 13 minutes | Serves 2

- 2 teaspoons rapeseed oil
- 4 eggs, whisked
- 3 tablespoons plain milk
- 1 teaspoon melted butter
- 1 red bell pepper, seeded and chopped
- 1 green bell pepper, seeded and chopped
- 1 white onion, finely chopped
- ½ cup baby spinach leaves, roughly chopped
- ½ cup Halloumi cheese, shaved
- flake salt and freshly ground black pepper, to taste

1. Preheat the air fryer to 180°C.
2. Grease a baking pan with rapeseed oil.
3. Put the remaining ingredients in the baking pan and stir well.
4. Transfer to the air fryer and bake for 13 minutes.
5. Serve warm.

Maple Milky Toast
Prep time: 10 minutes | Cook time: 40 minutes | Makes 12 cups

- 6 large eggs
- ¾ cup milk
- ¼ cup granulated sugar
- ¼ teaspoon ground cinnamon
- Pinch of ground nutmeg
- Pinch of salt
- 12 slices potato bread or country white bread
- 4 tablespoons unsalted butter
- Confectioners' sugar, for topping
- Pure maple syrup, for dipping

1. Preheat the air fryer to 190°C. Line a baking tray with greaseproof paper. Put the bangers on the baking tray and bake until lightly browned and cooked through, about 10 minutes.
2. Remove the pan from the air fryer with air fryer mitts and let cool slightly.
3. Meanwhile, combine the eggs, milk, granulated sugar, cinnamon, nutmeg and salt in a large bowl and whisk to combine. Cut each slice of bread into a 2-by-4-inch rectangle with a chef's knife, cutting off the crusts, then press the bread gently with your fingertips to flatten slightly.
4. Starting at a short end, roll each piece of bread around a banger link, pressing firmly with your fingers to seal the seam. Add the bread-wrapped bangers to the bowl with the egg mixture and let soak for 5 minutes.
5. Melt 2 tablespoons butter in a large nonstick frying pan over medium heat. Remove 6 of the bread-wrapped bangers from the egg mixture, letting the excess egg drip back into the bowl, then add to the frying pan. Cook, turning occasionally with a spatula, until golden brown, about 5 minutes.
6. Carefully remove the pigs in a blanket to kitchen paper using the spatula. Bunch up a paper towel and hold it with tongs to wipe out the frying pan.
7. Add the remaining 2 tablespoons butter to the frying pan and repeat with the other 6 bread-wrapped bangers.
8. Sprinkle the confectioners' sugar over the wrapped pigs in a blanket. Serve with maple syrup for dipping.

PICK A FILLING
9. Place ½ cup of one of the following ingredients in a medium bowl.
10. Softened cream cheese   Mashed banana
    Ricotta cheese   Marshmallow cream

ADD MIX-INS
11. Stir in ¼ cup total of the following ingredients (choose 1 or 2).
12. Stuff the Bread
13. Carefully cut four 1½-inch-thick slices from a loaf of challah bread with a serrated knife. With the bread slices flat on a cutting board, carefully cut a 2- to 3-inch-wide slit into the bottom edge of each bread slice with a paring knife to create a deep pocket. Put the filling in a resealable plastic bag and snip a corner. Pipe some filling into each pocket.

MAKE THE CUSTARD
14. Combine 2 eggs, 1 cup half-and-half, 1 tablespoon granulated sugar, 1 teaspoon vanilla, ½ teaspoon ground cinnamon, ¼ teaspoon ground nutmeg and a pinch of salt in a shallow bowl and whisk until combined.

COOK THE EGGY BREAD
15. Preheat the air fryer to 130°C. Dip a stuffed bread slice in the custard and soak 20 seconds per side; let the excess drip off and place on a plate. Repeat with the remaining bread slices.
16. Heat a large nonstick frying pan over medium heat. Melt 1 tablespoon butter in the frying pan, then add 2 stuffed bread slices and cook until browned, 4 to 5 minutes per side.
17. Place on a baking tray and keep warm in the air fryer. Bunch up a paper towel and hold it with tongs to wipe out the frying pan.

Egg in a Hole with Cheddar and Ham
Prep time: 5 minutes | Cook time: 5 minutes | Serves 1

- 1 slice bread
- 1 teaspoon butter, softened
- 1 egg
- Salt and pepper, to taste
- 1 tablespoon shredded Cheddar cheese
- 2 teaspoons diced ham

1. Preheat the air fryer to 170°C. Place a baking dish in the air fryer.
2. On a flat work surface, cut a hole in the center of the bread slice with a 2½-inch-diameter biscuit cutter.
3. Spread the butter evenly on each side of the bread slice and transfer to the baking dish.
4. Crack the egg into the hole and season as desired with salt and pepper. Scatter the shredded cheese and diced ham on top.
5. Bake in the preheated air fryer for 5 minutes until the bread is lightly browned and the egg is cooked to your preference.
6. Remove from the air fryer and serve hot.

Enticing Virginia Ham Pizza

Prep time: 10 minutes | Cook time: 15 minutes | serves 4

- Flour, for dusting the pan
- 1 disk fresh pizza dough, store-bought or from a pizza shop
- Olive oil
- Salt and Freshly ground black pepper, to taste
- 15 asparagus spears, woody ends trimmed
- 10 slices Virginia ham, torn into pieces
- 1 cup shredded Parmesan Cheese
- ½ cup shredded mozzarella
- 4 large eggs, each cracked into a separate small bowl or ramekin
- TOOLS/EQUIPMENT
- Grater
- 4 small bowls or ramekins
- Pizza stone or baking tray
- Basting brush (or paper towel)
- Large bowl
- Pizza cutter or knife

1. Prepare the air fryer. Position an air fryer rack in the middle of the air fryer. Prepare a pizza stone or baking tray by scattering flour lightly onto the surface. Preheat the air fryer to 200°C.
2. Prepare the dough. Shape the pizza dough into either a rustic rectangle or a traditional round, depending on the shape of your pan. Brush the dough lightly with oil, and season with salt and pepper.
3. Add the asparagus. Place a small amount of oil in your clean hands. In a large bowl, toss the asparagus spears with your hands, lightly coating them. Season the asparagus with salt and pepper, then arrange the asparagus in a sunburst pattern, with the tips pointing outward.
4. Bake the pizza and eggs and serve. Place in the air fryer and bake for 5 minutes. Remove from the air fryer, place ham all over the pizza, top with the cheeses, and slide each egg onto a separate quarter of the pizza.
5. Sprinkle the eggs with salt and pepper, and quickly return the pizza to the air fryer.
6. Bake for an additional 10 minutes, or until the crust is golden and the eggs are set to your liking. Cool slightly, slice into 4 wedges, and serve.

Bacon Whole Grain Tortilla Bar

Prep time: 10 minutes | Cook time: 12 minutes | serves 12

- 4 to 8 whole-grain (8- or 10-inch) tortillas
- 6 to 8 eggs, scrambled
- 2 cups tinned black beans, drained and rinsed
- 3 strips cooked bacon, crumbled
- 1 cup Greek yogurt or Soured cream
- 1 cup bite-size Coriander sprigs
- 1½ cups Salsa Fresca
- ½ cup orange, red, or green bell peppers, diced
- 1½ cups shredded sharp Cheddar or Parmesan Cheese
- 1½ cups diced avocado or No-Nonsense Guacamole
- Sriracha or Cholula chili sauce, for garnish
- TOOLS / EQUIPMENT
- Different-size
- Festive bowls
- Dish towel
- Box grater
- Colander
- Sauté pan
- tin foil

1. Preheat the air fryer to 190°C. Warm the tortillas.
2. Wrap a stack of 4 tortillas in tin foil and warm for 5 to 10 minutes. If you are preparing 8 tortillas, make 2 wrapped bundles. Wrap the warmed foil bundles in a dish towel to keep them toasty.
3. Serve the fillings and toppings in festive, colourful bowls.
4. Arrange them together on the table or counter, along with the towel-wrapped tortillas, and allow your guests to assemble their own burrito creations.

Pepper Spiced Broccoli Pastry

Prep time: 10 minutes | Cook time: 50 minutes | serves 6

- 1 frozen deep-dish piecrust
- 1½ cups whole milk
- 3 large eggs
- 1 tablespoon flour
- 1 tablespoon melted butter
- Dash salt
- Dash freshly ground black pepper
- ½ cup diced broccoli (frozen and thawed works best)
- 6 ounces (170 g) shredded Cheddar cheese
- TOOLS/EQUIPMENT
- Grater
- Deep-dish pie pan (if needed)
- Rimmed baking tray
- Large bowl
- Whisk
- Mixing spoon
- Knife

1. Preheat the air fryer. Preheat the air fryer to 190°C.
2. Prepare the crust. If your pie dough is not already in a disposable pie tin, press it into a deep-dish pie pan. Place the dough-filled pie pan on a rimmed baking tray.
3. Mix the ingredients. In a large bowl, whisk together the milk, eggs, flour, butter, salt, and pepper until combined. Stir in the broccoli and cheese.
4. Pour, bake, and serve. Pour the mixture into the pie pan, being careful not to overfill past three-quarters full.
5. Place the pie on the rimmed baking tray in the air fryer, and bake for 45 to 50 minutes, or until the quiche is puffed up and golden brown on top. Once removed from the air fryer, allow the quiche to set for at least 10 minutes before slicing and serving.

Havarti Asparagus Strata

Prep time: 10 minutes | Cook time: 14 to 19 minutes | Serves 4

- 6 asparagus spears, cut into 2-inch pieces
- 1 tablespoon water
- 2 slices whole-wheat bread, cut into ½-inch cubes
- 4 eggs
- 3 tablespoons whole milk
- 2 tablespoons chopped flat-leaf parsley
- ½ cup grated Havarti or Emmethaler
- Pinch salt
- Freshly ground black pepper, to taste
- Cooking spray

1. Preheat the air fryer to 170°C.
2. Add the asparagus spears and 1 tablespoon of water in a baking pan. Bake for 3 to 5 minutes until crisp-tender. Remove the asparagus from the pan and drain on kitchen paper. Spritz the pan with cooking spray.
3. Place the bread and asparagus in the pan.
4. Whisk together the eggs and milk in a medium mixing bowl until creamy. Fold in the parsley, cheese, salt, and pepper and stir to combine. Pour this mixture into the baking pan.
5. Bake for 11 to 14 minutes or until the eggs are set and the top is lightly browned.
6. Let cool for 5 minutes before slicing and serving.

Vanilla flavoured Peanut Bar

Prep time: 10 minutes | Cook time: 25 minutes | makes 16 bars

- Butter, for greasing
- 1¼ cups white and/or black sesame seeds
- ¾ cup unsweetened desiccated coconut
- ½ cup dried apricots, chopped
- ¼ teaspoon sea salt
- ¼ cup honey
- ⅓ cup crunchy peanut butter
- ¼ teaspoon pure vanilla extract
- TOOLS / EQUIPMENT
- 8-inch-square
- glass baking dish
- greaseproof paper
- Large bowl
- Small bowl
- Rubber spatula
- Wire cooling rack

1. Preheat the air fryer to 180°C. Prep the baking dish.
2. Butter an 8-inch-square glass baking dish, and line it with greaseproof paper long enough so that it extends beyond the dish by at least 2 inches on all sides. Cut slits at the corners so the parchment lays flat.
3. Mix the ingredients. In a large bowl, mix together the sesame seeds, coconut, apricots, and salt. In a small bowl, stir the honey, peanut butter, and vanilla extract. Add the honey mixture to the seed-and-fruit mixture, and stir well to combine.
4. Transfer the ingredients and bake.
5. Use a rubber spatula to scrape the mixture into the prepared baking dish, using the broad side of the spatula to press everything into an even layer. Bake until golden around the edges, 20 to 25 minutes. Transfer the baking dish to a wire cooling rack and let cool until firm, about 30 minutes.
6. Serve. Use the parchment tabs to lift the seeded block out of the baking dish—if it starts to crumble, let it cool longer. Using a sharp knife, cut 16 bars. Eat the fruit-seed-nut bars at room temperature. Store any leftovers in a sealed container at room temperature for up to 5 days.

Sugar Sprinkled Citrus Scones

Prep time: 10 minutes | Cook time: 20 minutes | serves 6

- 1½ cups plain flour, plus more for scattering
- ¼ cup sugar, plus more for sprinkling
- ½ tablespoon baking powder
- ⅛ teaspoon salt
- 6 tablespoons cold butter, cut into 12 pieces
- ½ cup dried blueberries
- ½ cup buttermilk, plus more for brushing the dough
- ½ tablespoon lemon zest
- TOOLS/EQUIPMENT
- Cutting board
- Knife
- Microplane or zester
- baking tray
- greaseproof paper or silicone baking mat
- Large bowl
- Whisk
- Mixing spoon
- Pastry cutter (optional)
- Chef's knife
- Pastry brush
- Toothpick

1. Preheat the air fryer. Preheat the air fryer to 200°C. Line a baking tray with greaseproof paper or a silicone baking mat
2. Mix the ingredients. In a large bowl, combine the flour, sugar, baking powder, and salt, and whisk together. Using a pastry cutter or your clean fingertips, work the butter into the flour mixture until it resembles pea-size balls.
3. Add the blueberries, stirring to combine. Add the buttermilk and lemon peel, and mix until a dough forms.
4. Prepare the dough. Scatter some flour onto a clean countertop. Transfer the dough to the floured counter, and use your hands to work it until all the flour is mixed in.
5. Shape the dough into a round disk. Break the dough into two pieces and shape into two 1-inch-high disks. Transfer the disks to the prepared baking tray. Using a chef's knife, cut each disk into 4 to 6 wedges. Space the wedges slightly apart.
6. Bake the scones. Brush the tops of the dough with a bit of buttermilk, and sprinkle with sugar and lemon zest.
7. Bake for 15 to 20 minutes, or until a toothpick inserted into the thickest part comes out mostly clean, and serve.

Cheesy Egg Bread Toast

Prep time: 10 minutes | Cook time: 20 minutes | serves 4

- 1 loaf ciabatta bread or French bread
- 4 to 6 large eggs
- 2 to 3 tablespoons heavy or single cream, divided
- 1 tablespoon chopped fresh parsley
- 1 tablespoon chopped scallion
- Salt and Freshly ground black pepper, to taste
- 2 to 3 tablespoons shredded Parmesan or Cheddar cheese
- TOOLS/EQUIPMENT
- Cutting board
- Knife
- baking tray

1. Preheat the air fryer. Preheat the air fryer to 180°C. Assemble the loaf.
2. Set the bread on a baking tray. Depending on the size of your bread loaf, cut 4 to 6 circles in the top ½ inch or so apart and about 2 inches in diameter. Scoop out the bread from the circles about an inch deep to form holes.
3. Fill the holes. Crack an egg into each hole, top each with ½ tablespoon of cream and some parsley, scallions, salt, and pepper. Sprinkle with the cheese.
4. Bake and serve. Bake for 20 minutes, or until the eggs are done to your liking. Cut into equal size pieces and serve.

Cinnamon Applesauce Porridge

Prep time: 10 minutes | Cook time: 30 minutes | serves 6

- 2 cups old-fashioned oats
- 2 teaspoons ground cinnamon
- Pinch salt
- 1 heaping cup peeled, diced Granny Smith apples
- ¾ cup Cinnamon Applesauce
- ¼ cup whole milk
- ¼ cup grape seed or olive oil
- 2 large eggs
- 3 tablespoons maple syrup, plus more for drizzling
- TOOLS/EQUIPMENT
- Cutting board
- Knife
- Peeler
- 8-by-8-inch baking dish
- Large bowl
- Mixing spoon
- Nonstick cooking spray

1. Preheat the air fryer. Preheat the air fryer to 180°C. Spray an 8-by-8-inch baking dish with cooking spray, and set aside.
2. Mix the ingredients. In a large bowl, combine all the ingredients and stir until fully blended.
3. Bake the Porridge and serve. Scrape the batter into the prepared baking dish and spread evenly. Bake for 30 minutes, or until golden brown on top.
4. Allow to sit for 5 minutes before serving. Drizzle with additional maple syrup if desired.

Sweet and Yummy Milk Pancake

Prep time: 5 minutes | Cook time: 15 minutes | serves 4

- ¾ cup plain flour
- ¾ cup whole milk
- 4 eggs, lightly beaten
- 2 tablespoons cane sugar
- Pinch freshly grated nutmeg
- ¼ teaspoon sea salt
- 4 tablespoons butter, divided into 4 pats
- Confectioners' sugar, for dusting
- Lemon wedges, for serving
- Delicious additions
- Jam
- Cinnamon sugar
- Fresh berries
- Stewed apples
- Whipped cream or crème fraîche
- TOOLS / EQUIPMENT
- Small, shallow ramekins
- baking tray
- Blender

1. Preheat the air fryer to 425°F(218°C). Prep the ramekins.
2. Arrange the ramekins on a rimmed baking tray, and place in the air fryer to heat.

BLEND THE INGREDIENTS.

3. In a blender, mix the flour, milk, eggs, sugar, nutmeg, and salt until frothy.
4. Butter the ramekins. When the ramekins are hot, add a pat of butter to each and, using pot holders for protection, swirl to coat. Butter should foam. Replace in air fryer until fully melted.
5. Bake the Dutch Babies. Remove baking tray from the air fryer. Divide the batter evenly among the ramekins, and bake until the Dutch Babies are puffed and golden brown, 10 to 15 minutes.
6. Serve.

Delicious Butter Muffins

Prep time: 10 minutes | Cook time: 10 minutes | serves 6

FOR THE MUFFINS
- Nonstick cooking spray
- 1¾ cups flour
- 1½ teaspoons baking powder
- 1½ teaspoons Mixed Spice
- ¼ to ½ cup butter, melted
- ½ teaspoon salt
- 1 cup pumpkin purée (not pumpkin pie filling)
- ¾ cup sugar
- ⅓ cup vegetable oil
- 1 large egg
- FOR THE COATING
- ⅓ cup sugar
- 1 tablespoon Mixed Spice
- ¼ to ½ cup butter, melted
- TOOLS/EQUIPMENT
- Mini muffin pan
- 1 medium bowl, 1 large bowl, and 2 small bowls
- Mixing spoon
- Toothpick
- greaseproof paper
- Wire rack (optional)

1. Preheat the air fryer. Preheat the air fryer to 180°C, and spray a mini muffin pan with cooking spray.
2. Mix the dry ingredients. In a medium bowl, mix together the flour, baking powder, Mixed Spice , and salt. Set aside.
3. Mix the wet ingredients. In a large bowl, combine the pumpkin purée, sugar, oil, and egg. Add the dry ingredients to the wet ingredients, and stir until combined.
4. Bake the muffins. Fill the muffin cups three-quarters full with batter. Bake for 8 to 9 minutes, or until a toothpick inserted into the center of a muffin comes out clean.
5. Prepare the coating. In a small bowl, mix the sugar and Mixed Spice . Set this bowl next to your bowl of melted butter.
6. Coat and serve. Transfer the muffins onto greaseproof paper. While still hot, dip them one by one into the melted butter, then immediately roll in the sugar mixture, coating the muffin entirely. Enjoy hot or place on a wire rack to cool.

Sweet and Sour Tomato Egg frying pan
Prep time: 10 minutes | Cook time: 20 minutes | serves 4

- 1 onion, chopped
- 2 tablespoons olive oil
- 2 garlic cloves, chopped
- 1 (28-ounce) can tomatoes
- 1 tablespoon za'atar
- 2 teaspoons cumin seeds, toasted and ground in a mortar and pestle
- flake salt and freshly ground black pepper, to taste
- 4 eggs
- ¼ cup fresh Coriander leaves, for garnish
- ⅔ cup Greek yogurt or Soured cream
- Crusty bread, torn, for serving
- Delicious additions
- Chickpeas
- Artichoke hearts
- Feta
- TOOLS / EQUIPMENT
- Toaster air fryer
- Mortar and pestle
- Large
- Enameled frying pan
- Wooden spoon

1. Preheat the air fryer to 190°C. Cook the onion and garlic.
2. In a large enameled frying pan over medium heat, sauté the onion in olive oil for 3 to 5 minutes. Add the chopped garlic, and cook for another minute.
3. Add the tomatoes and aromatics. Add the tomatoes, and bring to a simmer. Add the za'atar and cumin, season with salt and pepper, and simmer uncovered for a few minutes, until the sauce thickens.
4. Break the tomatoes into chunks using the edge of a wooden spoon. Taste and adjust seasoning as needed.
5. Add the eggs. Use the wooden spoon to make four nests in the sauce and crack an egg into each. Season the eggs with salt and pepper, and transfer the frying pan to the air fryer, cooking for 7 to 10 minutes, or until the eggs are just set.
6. Serve from the frying pan on a trivet at the table. Season with salt and pepper to taste, and garnish with fresh Coriander and a few dollops of yogurt. Serve with the bread to mop up the sauce and yolks.

Vanilla flavoured Milky Butter Cake
Prep time: 10 minutes | Cook time: 50 minutes | serves 6

- FOR THE CAKE
- Nonstick cooking spray
- 2 cups plain flour
- 2½ tablespoons baking powder
- ½ teaspoon salt
- 3 overripe bananas
- 2 cups granulated sugar
- 1 cup whole milk
- ½ cup melted and cooled butter
- 2 large eggs
- 1 teaspoon vanilla extract
- FOR THE CRUMB TOPPING
- 1½ cups Demerara sugar
- 1½ cups plain flour
- 6 tablespoons cold butter, cut into 12 pieces
- TOOLS/EQUIPMENT
- Cutting board
- Knife
- 13-by-9-inch baking dish
- 1 small, 1 large, and 1 medium bowl
- Whisk
- Potato masher
- Pastry cutter (optional)
- Toothpick
- Preheat the air fryer.

1. Preheat the air fryer to 180°C. Spray a 13-by-9-inch baking dish with cooking spray. Set aside. Mix the dry ingredients.
2. In a small bowl, whisk together the flour, baking powder, and salt. Set aside. Mix the batter.
3. In a large bowl, mash the bananas with a potato masher until mushy. Add the granulated sugar, milk, butter, eggs, and vanilla, and stir until fully combined. Add the flour mixture, and mix until fully combined. Scrape the batter into the prepared baking dish.
4. Add the topping. In a medium bowl, combine the Demerara sugar, flour, and butter. Using a pastry cutter or your fingertips, blend until the mixture resembles crumbs. Sprinkle the topping over the batter.
5. Bake the cake and serve. Bake for 45 to 50 minutes, or until a toothpick inserted into the middle comes out dry. Allow the cake to cool, then cut into squares and serve.

Chapter 3
Poultry

Fry Balsamic Chicken Strips

Prep time: 10 minutes | Cook time: 18 minutes | Serves 4

- 1 pound (454 g) chicken breasts, cut into strips
- 2 tomatoes, cubed
- 1 green chili pepper, cut into stripes
- ½ teaspoon cumin
- 2 spring onions, sliced
- 2 tablespoon olive oil
- 1 tablespoon yellow mustard
- ½ teaspoon ginger powder
- 2 tablespoon fresh Coriander, chopped
- Salt and black pepper to taste

1. Heat olive oil in a deep pan over medium heat and sauté mustard, spring onions, ginger powder, cumin, and green chili pepper for 2 to 3 minutes.
2. Stir in tomatoes, Coriander, and salt; set aside. Preheat the air fryer to 190°C. Season the chicken with salt and pepper, and place in the greased air fryer basket or wire rack.
3. Air Fry for 15 minutes, shaking once. Top with the sauce and serve.

Crunchy Coconut Chicken with Berry Sauce

Prep time: 5 minutes | Cook time: 16 minutes | Serves 4

- 2 cups coconut flakes
- 4 chicken breasts, cut into strips
- ½ cup cornflour
- Salt and black pepper to taste
- 2 eggs, beaten

1. Preheat air fryer to 180°C. Mix salt, pepper, and cornflour in a bowl. Line a frying basket with greaseproof paper.
2. Dip the chicken first in the cornflour, then into the eggs, and finally, coat with coconut flakes.
3. Arrange in the air fryer and Bake for 16 minutes, flipping once until crispy. Serve with berry sauce.

Avocado and Mango Chicken Breasts

Prep time: 10 minutes | Cook time: 14 minutes | Serves 2

- 2 chicken breasts
- 1 mango, chopped
- 1 avocado, sliced
- 1 red pepper, chopped
- 1 tablespoon balsamic vinegar
- 2 tablespoon olive oil
- 2 garlic cloves, minced
- ½ teaspoon dried oregano
- 1 teaspoon mustard powder
- Salt and black pepper to taste

1. In a bowl, mix garlic, olive oil, and balsamic vinegar. Add in the breasts, cover, and marinate for 2 hours.
2. Preheat the fryer to 180°C. Place the chicken in the frying basket and Air Fry for 12 to 14 minutes, flipping once.
3. Top with avocado, mango, and red pepper. Drizzle with balsamic vinegar and serve.

Baked Coconut and Mango Chicken Thighs

Prep time: 5 minutes | Cook time: 14 minutes | Serves 4

- 1 tablespoon curry powder
- 4 tablespoon mango chutney
- Salt and black pepper to taste
- ¾ cup coconut, shredded
- 1 pound (454 g) chicken thighs

1. Preheat air fryer to 200°C. In a bowl, mix curry powder, mango chutney, salt, and black pepper.
2. Brush the thighs with the glaze and roll the chicken thighs in desiccated coconut.
3. Grease a baking dish with cooking spray and arrange the thing in. Bake them in the air fryer for 12 to 14 minutes, turning once, until golden brown.

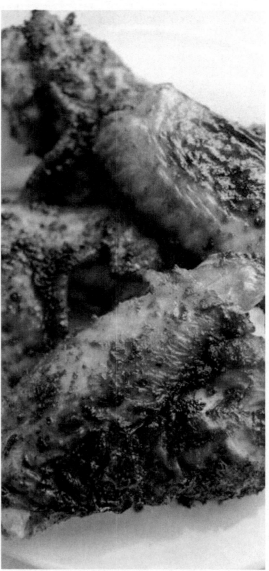

Lemony-Fried Chicken Legs with Herbs

Prep time: 5 minutes | Cook time: 18 minutes | Serves 4

- 4 chicken legs
- 2 lemons, halved
- 1 tablespoon garlic powder
- ½ teaspoon dried oregano
- ⅓ cup olive oil
- Salt and black pepper to taste

1. Preheat the air fryer to 180°C. Brush the chicken legs with olive oil. Sprinkle with lemon juice and arrange in the frying basket.
2. In a bowl, mix oregano, garlic powder, salt, and pepper.
3. Scatter the seasoning mixture over the chicken and Bake the legs in the air fryer for 14 to 16 minutes, shaking once.

Sesame Chicken with Sweet Wasabi

Prep time: 5 minutes | Cook time: 16 minutes | Serves 2

- 2 tablespoon wasabi
- 1 tablespoon agave syrup
- 2 teaspoon black sesame seeds
- Salt and black pepper to taste
- 2 chicken breasts, cut into large chunks

1. In a bowl, mix wasabi, agave syrup, sesame seed, salt, and pepper. Rub the mixture onto the breasts.
2. Arrange the breasts on a greased frying basket and cook for 16 minutes, turning once halfway through.

Cumin Mustard Chicken Strips

Prep time: 10 minutes | Cook time: 23 minutes | Serves 4

- 1 pound (454 g) chicken breasts, cut into strips
- 2 tomatoes, cubed
- 1 green chili pepper, cut into stripes
- ½ teaspoon cumin
- 2 spring onions, sliced
- 2 tablespoon olive oil
- 1 tablespoon yellow mustard
- ½ teaspoon ginger powder
- 2 tablespoon fresh Coriander, chopped
- Salt and black pepper to taste

1. In a bowl, mix the lemon juice, 2 tablespoon of the olive oil, Cranberry Juice, and salt and whisk with a fork. Add in the tomatoes, spring onions, radishes, cucumber, fresh mint and toss to coat.
2. Reserve. Preheat your Air Fryer to 190°C. Combine the paprika, garlic powder, salt, black pepper, and cayenne pepper in a small bowl, then rub the mixture all over the turkey. Put the turkey in the greased fryer basket and spray with olive oil, then air fry for 15 minutes.
3. Turn it over and spray it again, then cook for 10 to 15 more minutes. Remove the turkey and let it sit for 5 to 8 minutes before slicing. Transfer the salad to a serving dish and top with pita crackers. Serve the turkey with the salad and enjoy!

Chicken Bowl with Peppers and Corn

Prep time: 10 minutes | Cook time: 18 minutes | Serves 4

- 4 chicken breasts, cubed
- 1 can sweet corn
- 1 can black beans, rinsed and drained
- 1 cup red and green peppers, stripes, cooked
- 1 tablespoon vegetable oil
- 1 teaspoon chili powder

1. Coat the chicken with salt, black pepper, and a bit of oil. Air Fry for 15 minutes at 190°C.
2. In a deep frying pan, pour 1 tablespoon of oil and stir in chili powder, corn, peppers, and beans.
3. Add a little bit of hot water and keep stirring for 3 minutes. Transfer the veggies to a serving platter and top with the fried chicken.

Honey Chicken Wings with Chili Sauce

Prep time: 10 minutes | Cook time: 16 minutes | Serves 4

- 1 pound (454 g) chicken wingettes
- 1 tablespoon fresh Coriander, chopped
- Salt and black pepper to taste
- 1 tablespoon roasted peanuts, chopped
- ½ tablespoon apple cider vinegar
- 1 garlic clove, minced
- ½ tablespoon chili sauce
- 1 ginger, minced
- 1 ½ tablespoon soy sauce
- ½ tablespoon honey

1. Preheat air fryer to 180°C . Season chicken wingettes with salt and pepper. In a bowl, mix ginger, garlic, chili sauce, honey, soy sauce, Coriander, and vinegar.
2. Cover chicken with the mixture. Transfer to the air fryer basket or wire rack and cook for 14 to 16 minutes, shaking once.
3. Serve sprinkled with peanuts.

Sweet Mustard Chicken Thighs

Prep time: 5 minutes | Cook time: 18 minutes | Serves 4

- 4 chicken thighs, skin-on
- 1 tablespoon honey
- 1 teaspoon Dijon mustard
- Salt and garlic powder to taste

1. In a bowl, mix honey, mustard, garlic powder, and salt.
2. Brush the thighs with the mixture and Air Fry them for 16 minutes at 200°C, turning once halfway through. Serve hot.

Fry Sliced Golden aubergine with Garlic

Prep time: 10 minutes | Cook time: 12 minutes | Serves 4

- 2 aubergines, sliced
- 2 cups bread crumbs
- 1 teaspoon Italian seasoning
- 1 cup flour Salt to taste
- 4 eggs
- 2 gave cloves, sliced
- 2 tablespoon fresh parsley, chopped

1. Preheat air fryer to 200°C. In a bowl, beat the eggs with salt. In a separate bowl, mix breadcrumbs and Italian seasoning.
2. In a third bowl, pour the flour. Dip aubergine steaks in the flour, followed by a dip in the eggs, and finally, coat in the breadcrumbs.
3. Place in the greased air fryer basket or wire rack and Air Fry for 10 to 12 minutes, flipping once. Remove to a platter and sprinkle with garlic and parsley to serve. enjoy!

Tamarind Chicken Wings with Sweet Chili

Prep time: 10 minutes | Cook time: 14 minutes | Serves 4

- 1 pound (454 g) chicken wings
- 1 teaspoon ginger root powder
- 1 tablespoon tamarind powder
- ¼ cup sweet chili sauce

1. Preheat air fryer to 200°C. Rub the chicken wings with tamarind and ginger root powders.
2. Spray with cooking spray and place in the air fryer basket or wire rack. Cook for 6 minutes.
3. Slide-out the air fryer basket or wire rack and cover with sweet chili sauce; cook for 8 more minutes. Serve warm.

Crispy Chicken Tenderloins

Prep time: 5 minutes | Cook time: 18 minutes | Serves 4

- 8 chicken tenderloins
- 2 tablespoon butters, melted
- 1 cup seasoned breadcrumbs

1. Preheat air fryer to 190°C. Dip the chicken in the eggs, then coat with the seasoned crumbs.
2. Coat the air fryer basket or wire rack with some butter and place in the chicken.
3. Brush with the remaining butter and cook for 14 to 16 minutes, shaking once halfway through. Serve with your favourite dip.

Turmeric Chicken Fillets with Sweet Chili

Prep time: 5 minutes | Cook time: 18 minutes | Serves 4

- 2 chicken breasts, halved
- Salt and black pepper to taste
- ¼ cup sweet chili sauce
- 1 teaspoon taste

1. Preheat air fryer to 200°C. In a bowl, add salt, black pepper, sweet chili sauce, and turmeric; mix well.
2. Lightly brush the chicken with the mixture and place it in the frying basket. Air Fry for 12 to 14 minutes, turning once halfway through. Serve with a side of steamed greens.

Honey-Glazed Turkey with Thyme

Prep time: 10 minutes | Cook time: 30 minutes | Serves 4

- 1½ pounds (680 g) turkey tenderloins
- ¼ cup honey
- 2 tablespoon Dijon mustard
- ½ teaspoon dried thyme
- ½ teaspoon garlic powder
- ½ onion powder
- 1 tablespoon olive oil
- ½ tablespoon spicy brown mustard
- Salt and black pepper to taste

1. Preheat air fryer to 190°C. Combine the honey, mustard, thyme, garlic powder, and onion powder in a bowl to make a paste. Season the turkey with salt and pepper, then spread the honey paste all over it.
2. Put the turkey in the fryer basket and spray with olive oil, then air fry for 15 minutes. Turn it over and spray again before frying for 10 to 15 more minutes. Remove the turkey, cover loosely with foil and let stand 10 minutes before slicing. Serve and enjoy!

Easy Vegetable Croquettes

Prep time: 15 minutes | Cook time: 32 minutes | Serves 4

- 1 pound (454 g) red potatoes
- 1¼ cups milk
- Salt to taste
- 3 tablespoon butters
- 2 teaspoon olive oil
- 1 red bell pepper, chopped
- ½ cup baby spinach, chopped
- 1½ pounds (680 g) mushrooms, chopped
- 1½ pounds (680 g) broccoli florets, chopped
- 1 green onion, sliced
- 1 red onion, chopped
- 2 garlic cloves, minced
- 1 carrot, grated
- ⅓ cup flour
- 2 eggs, beaten
- 1½ cups breadcrumbs

1. Cover the potatoes with salted water in a pot over medium heat and cook for about 15 to 18 minutes. Drain and place in a bowl. Add in 2 tablespoons of butter, 1 cup of milk, and salt.
2. Mash with a potato masher. In a food processor, place onion, garlic, bell pepper, broccoli, mushrooms, green onion, spinach, olive oil, salt, and remaining milk and pulse until a breadcrumb texture is formed. Mix with mashed potatoes.
3. Using your hands, create oblong balls out of the mixture and place them on a baking tray in a single layer. Refrigerate for 30 minutes. Preheat air fryer to 200°C. Take 3 separate bowls, pour breadcrumbs in one, flour in another, and eggs in a third bowl.
4. Remove the croquettes from the fridge. Dredge the croquettes in flour, then in the eggs, and finally in the crumbs.
5. Arrange them on the greased frying basket without overlapping. Air Fry for 12 to 14 minutes, shaking once. Remove to a wire rack. Let cool and serve. enjoy!

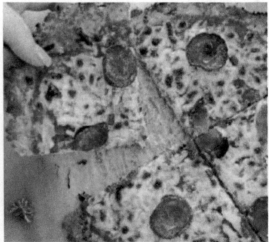

Chicken Traybake with Cherry Tomatoes

Prep time: 10 minutes | Cook time: 25 minutes | Serves 4

- 1 pound (454 g) chicken drumsticks, skin on and bone-in
- 3 shallots, quartered
- Salt and black pepper to taste
- 1 tablespoon cayenne pepper
- 1 pound (454 g) baby potatoes, halved ½ teaspoon garlic powder
- 2 tablespoon olive oil 1 cup cherry tomatoes

1. Preheat air fryer to 180°C . Place the chicken in a baking tray and add in shallots, potatoes, oil, garlic powder, salt, and pepper; toss to coat.
2. Place the tray in the fryer and bake for 18 to 20 minutes, shaking once. Slide the air fryer basket or wire rack out and add in the cherry tomatoes. Cook for another 5 minutes until charred.

Cream Polenta Chips

Prep time: 10 minutes | Cook time: 16 minutes | Serves 4

- 2 cups milk
- 1 cup instant polenta
- Salt and black pepper to taste
- 2 tablespoon fresh thyme, chopped

1. Line a baking dish with greaseproof paper. Pour 2 cups of milk and 2 cups of water into a saucepan and let simmer.
2. Keep whisking as you pour in the polenta. Continue to whisk until polenta thickens and bubbles; season to taste.
3. Add polenta into the lined dish and spread out. Refrigerate for 45 minutes. Slice the cold polenta into batons.
4. Arrange the chips on the greased frying basket and Air Fry for 14 to 16 minutes at 190°C, turning once halfway.

Fry Crispy and Creamy Runner Beans

Prep time: 10 minutes | Cook time: 15 minutes | Serves 4

- 1 cup panko breadcrumbs
- 2 eggs, beaten
- ½ cup Parmesan cheese, grated
- ½ cup flour
- 1 teaspoon cayenne pepper
- 1½ pounds (680 g) Runner Beans
- 1 cup tomato pasta sauce
- Salt and black pepper to taste

1. Preheat air fryer to 200°C. In a bowl, mix breadcrumbs, Parmesan cheese, cayenne pepper, salt, and pepper.
2. Coat the Runner Beans in the flour, followed by the beaten egg and finally the Parmesan-panko crumbs.
3. Air Fry in the fryer for 15 minutes, turning once halfway through. Serve with tomato sauce. enjoy

Classic Crispy Sweet Potato French chips

Prep time: 10 minutes | Cook time: 25 minutes | Serves 4

- ½ teaspoon salt
- ½ teaspoon garlic powder
- ½ teaspoon chili powder
- ¼ teaspoon cumin
- 3 tablespoon olive oil
- 4 sweet potatoes, cut into thick strips

1. In a bowl, mix salt, garlic powder, chili powder, and cumin and whisk in olive oil. Coat the strips in the mixture and place them in the frying basket.
2. Air Fry for 20 minutes at 190°C, shaking once, until crispy. Traditional Jacket Potatoes 1 pound (454 g) potatoes 2 garlic cloves, minced Salt and black pepper to taste 1 teaspoon dried rosemary 2 teaspoon butter, melted.
3. Preheat air fryer to 180°C . Prick the potatoes with a fork. Place them in the greased frying basket and Bake for 23 to 25 minutes, turning once halfway through.
4. Remove and cut in half. Drizzle with melted butter and season with salt and black pepper. Sprinkle with rosemary and serve. enjoy!

Fry aubergine and courgette Chips
Prep time: 5 minutes | Cook time: 12 minutes | Serves 4

- 1 large aubergine, cut into strips
- 1 courgette, cut into strips
- ½ cup cornflour
- 3 tablespoon olive oil
- Salt to season

1. Preheat air fryer to 200°C. In a bowl, stir in cornflour, salt, pepper, olive oil, aubergines, and courgette.
2. Place the coated veggies in the greased frying basket and Air Fry for 12 minutes, shaking once. enjoy!

Crispy Rosemary Chickpeas
Prep time: 10 minutes | Cook time: 12 minutes | Serves 4

- 1 (15-ounces/ 425 g) can chickpeas, rinsed
- 1 tablespoon butter, melted
- ½ teaspoon dried rosemary
- ¼ teaspoon turmeric

1. Preheat air fryer to 190°C. In a bowl, combine together chickpeas, butter, rosemary, turmeric, and salt; toss to coat.
2. Place the in the greased frying basket and Air Fry for 6 minutes. Shake, and cook for 6 more minutes until crispy. enjoy!

Roasted Pumpkin and Red Bell Peppery
Prep time: 10 minutes | Cook time: 25 minutes | Serves 4

- 1 pound (454 g) pumpkin, peeled and cubed
- 2 red bell peppers, diced
- 2 shallots, quartered
- 1 red chili pepper, minced
- 1 teaspoon ground caraway seeds
- 1 cup orzo
- Salt and black pepper to taste

1. Preheat air fryer to 190°C. In a bowl, place the pumpkin, bell peppers, shallots, chili pepper, ground caraway seeds, salt, and pepper; toss to coat. Transfer to the greased frying basket.
2. Bake for 20 to 25 minutes, shaking once until golden. Place a pot filled with salted water over medium heat and bring to a boil. Add in the orzo and cook for 4 minutes.
3. Drain and place on a serving platter. Spread the baked pumpkin all over. Serve and enjoy!

Chapter 4
Beef lamb and Pork

Crusted Pork Chops

Prep Time: 8 minutes |Cooking Time: 15 minutes| Servings: 4

- 2 Pork chops
- 3 tbsp. Olive oil
- 1 tbsp. Chopped rosemary
- Salt and pepper to taste
- 1 tbsp. fennel

1. In a bowl, add in the pork chops with the salt, fennel, Oil, pepper and the rosemary
2. Stir and ensure the pork chops coat well
3. Arrange the chops to your Air fryer and Cook for 15 minutes at 200°C
4. Share the chops between plates and serve

Pork Kebab with Yogurt Sauce

Prep time: 25 minutes | Cook time: 12 minutes | Serves 4

- 2 teaspoons olive oil
- ½ pound (227g) ground pork
- ½ pound (227g) minced beef
- 1 egg, whisked
- Sea salt and ground black pepper, to taste
- 1 teaspoon paprika
- 2 garlic cloves, minced
- 1 teaspoon dried marjoram
- 1 teaspoon mustard seeds
- ½ teaspoon celery seeds
- Yogurt Sauce:
- 2 tablespoons olive oil
- 2 tablespoons fresh lemon juice
- Sea salt, to taste
- ¼ teaspoon red pepper flakes, crushed
- ½ cup full-fat yogurt
- 1 teaspoon dried dill weed

1. Spritz the sides and bottom of the cooking basket with 2 teaspoons of olive oil.
2. In a mixing dish, thoroughly combine the ground pork, beef, egg, salt, black pepper, paprika, garlic, marjoram, mustard seeds, and celery seeds.
3. Form the mixture into kebabs and transfer them to the greased cooking basket. Cook at 180°C for 11 to 12 minutes, turning them over once or twice. In the meantime, mix all the sauce ingredients and place in the refrigerator until ready to serve. Serve the pork kebabs with the yogurt sauce on the side. Enjoy!

Cheesy Pork Beef Casserole

Prep time: 20 minutes | Cook time: 10 minutes | Serves 4

- 1 pound (454 g) lean ground pork
- ½ pound (227g) minced beef
- ¼ cup tomato purée
- Sea salt and ground black pepper, to taste
- 1 teaspoon smoked paprika
- ½ teaspoon dried oregano
- 1 teaspoon dried basil
- 1 teaspoon dried rosemary
- 2 eggs
- 1 cup Cottage cheese, crumbled, at room temperature
- ½ cup Cotija cheese, shredded

1. Lightly grease a casserole dish with a nonstick cooking oil. Add the ground meat to the bottom of your casserole dish.
2. Add the tomato purée. Sprinkle with salt, black pepper, paprika, oregano, basil, and rosemary.
3. In a mixing bowl, whisk the egg with cheese. Place on top of the ground meat mixture. Place a piece of foil on top.
4. Bake in the preheated Air fryer at 180°C for 10 minutes; remove the foil and cook an additional 6 minutes.

Savory Sirloin Steak

Prep time: 20 minutes | Cook time: 14 minutes | Serves 2

- 1 pound (454 g) Sirloin steak, cut meat from bones in 2 pieces
- ½ teaspoon ground black pepper
- 1 teaspoon cayenne pepper
- ½ teaspoon salt
- 1 teaspoon garlic powder
- ½ teaspoon dried thyme
- ½ teaspoon dried marjoram
- 1 teaspoon Dijon mustard
- 1 tablespoon butter, melted

1. Sprinkle the Sirloin steak with all the seasonings.
2. Spread the mustard and butter evenly over the meat.
3. Cook in the preheated Air fryer at 200°C for 12 to 14 minutes.
4. Taste for doneness with a meat thermometer and serve immediately.

Cheese Wine Pork Cutlets

Prep time: 20 minutes | Cook time: 15 minutes | Serves 2

- 1 cup water
- 1 cup red wine
- 1 tablespoon sea salt
- 2 pork cutlets
- ¼ cup almond meal
- ¼ cup flaxseed meal
- ½ teaspoon baking powder
- 1 teaspoon shallot powder
- ½ teaspoon porcini powder
- Sea salt and ground black pepper, to taste
- 1 egg
- ¼ cup yogurt
- 1 teaspoon brown mustard
- ⅓ cup Parmesan cheese, grated

1. In a large ceramic dish, combine the water, wine and salt. Add the pork cutlets and put for 1 hour in the refrigerator.
2. In a shallow bowl, mix the almond meal, flaxseed meal, baking powder, shallot powder, porcini powder, salt, and ground pepper. In another bowl, whisk the eggs with yogurt and mustard.
3. In a third bowl, place the grated Parmesan cheese.
4. Dip the pork cutlets in the seasoned flour mixture and toss evenly; then, in the egg mixture. Finally, roll them over the grated Parmesan cheese.
5. Spritz the bottom of the cooking basket with cooking oil. Add the breaded pork cutlets and cook at 200°C and for 10 minutes.
6. Flip and cook for 5 minutes more on the other side. Serve warm.

Cheesy Pork Tenderloin

Prep time: 25 minutes | Cook time: 22 minutes | Serves 4

- 2 tablespoons olive oil
- 2 pounds (907 g) pork tenderloin, cut into serving-size pieces
- 1 teaspoon coarse sea salt
- ½ teaspoon freshly ground pepper
- ¼ teaspoon chili powder
- 1 teaspoon dried marjoram
- 1 tablespoon mustard
- 1 cup Ricotta cheese
- 1½ cups chicken broth

1. Start by preheating your Air fryer to 180°C.
2. Heat the olive oil in a pan over medium-high heat. Once hot, cook the pork for 6 to 7 minutes, flipping it to ensure even cooking.
3. Arrange the pork in a lightly greased casserole dish. Season with salt, black pepper, chili powder, and marjoram.
4. In a mixing dish, thoroughly combine the mustard, cheese, and chicken broth. Pour the mixture over the pork chops in the casserole dish.
5. Bake for another 15 minutes or until bubbly and heated through. Bon appétit!

Onion Pork Kebabs

Prep time: 22 minutes | Cook time: 18 minutes | Serves 3

- 2 tablespoons tomato purée
- ½ fresh serrano, minced
- ⅓ teaspoon paprika
- 1 pound (454 g) pork, ground
- ½ cup spring onions, finely chopped
- 3 cloves garlic, peeled and finely minced
- 1 teaspoon ground black pepper, or more to taste
- 1 teaspoon salt, or more to taste

1. Thoroughly combine all ingredients in a mixing dish. Then, form your mixture into banger shapes.
2. Cook for 18 minutes at 180°C. Mound salad on a serving platter, top with air-fried kebabs and serve warm. Bon appétit!

Savory Pork Loin

Prep time: 50 minutes | Cook time: 16 minutes | Serves 3

- 1 teaspoon Celtic sea salt
- ½ teaspoon black pepper, freshly cracked
- ¼ cup red wine
- 2 tablespoons mustard
- 2 garlic cloves, minced
- 1 pound (454 g) pork top loin
- 1 tablespoon Italian herb seasoning blend

1. In a ceramic bowl, mix the salt, black pepper, red wine, mustard, and garlic. Add the pork top loin and let it marinate at least 30 minutes.
2. Spritz the sides and bottom of the cooking basket with a nonstick cooking spray.
3. Place the pork top loin in the air fryer basket or wire rack; sprinkle with the Italian herb seasoning blend.
4. Cook the pork tenderloin at 190°C for 10 minutes. Flip halfway through, spraying with cooking oil and cook for 5 to 6 minutes more. Serve immediately.

Cheese Pork Meatballs

Prep time: 15 minutes | Cook time: 7 minutes | Serves 3

- 1 pound (454 g) ground pork
- 1 tablespoon coconut aminos
- 1 teaspoon garlic, minced
- 2 tablespoons spring onions, finely chopped
- ½ cup scratchings
- ½ cup Parmesan cheese, preferably freshly grated

1. Combine the ground pork, coconut aminos, garlic, and spring onions in a mixing dish. Mix until everything is well incorporated.
2. Form the mixture into small meatballs.
3. In a shallow bowl, mix the scratchings and grated Parmesan cheese. Roll the meatballs over the Parmesan mixture.
4. Cook at 190°C for 3 minutes; shake the air fryer basket or wire rack and cook an additional 4 minutes or until meatballs are browned on all sides. Bon appétit!

Air Fried Pork Chop

Prep time: 22 minutes | Cook time: 18 minutes | Serves 6

- 2 tablespoons vermouth
- 6 center-cut loin pork chops
- ½ tablespoon fresh basil, minced
- ⅓ teaspoon freshly ground black pepper, or more to taste
- 2 tablespoons whole grain mustard
- 1 teaspoon fine flake salt

1. Toss pork chops with other ingredients until they are well coated on both sides.
2. Air-fry your chops for 18 minutes at 200°C, turning once or twice.
3. Mound your favourite salad on a serving plate; top with pork chops and enjoy!

Herbed Lamb Chops

Prep Time: 7 minutes Cooking Time: 8 minutes Servings: 2

- 1 tbsp. fresh lemon juice
- 1 tbsp. olive oil
- 1 tsp. dried rosemary
- 1 tsp. dried thyme
- 1 tsp. Dried oregano
- ½ tsp. Ground cumin
- ½ tsp. ground coriander
- Salt and ground black pepper, as required
- 4 (4-oz.) lamb chops

1. In a bowl, mix well the lemon juice, oil, herbs, and spices. Add the chops and coat evenly with the herb mixture.
2. Refrigerate to marinate for about 1 hour.
3. Set the temperature of the Air fryer to 190°C and time to 7 minutes.
4. Grease a air fryer basket or wire rack. Arrange chops into the prepared air fryer basket or wire rack in a single layer.
5. Flip once halfway through
6. Remove from the Air fryer and transfer the chops onto plates.
7. Serve hot.

Cheesy Pork banger Meatball

Prep time: 20 minutes | Cook time: 10 minutes | Serves 4

- 1 pound (454 g) pork banger meat
- 1 shallot, finely chopped
- 2 garlic cloves, finely minced
- ½ teaspoon fine sea salt
- ¼ teaspoon ground black pepper, or more to taste
- ¾ teaspoon paprika
- ½ cup Parmesan cheese, preferably freshly grated
- ½ jar no-sugar-added marinara sauce

1. Mix all of the above ingredients, except the marinara sauce, in a large-sized dish, until everything is well incorporated.
2. Shape into meatballs. Air-fry them at 180°C for 10 minutes; pause the Air fryer, shake them up and cook for additional 6 minutes or until the balls are no longer pink in the middle.
3. Meanwhile, heat the marinara sauce over a medium flame. Serve the pork banger meatballs with marinara sauce. Bon appétit!

Greens with Shallot and Bacon

Prep time: 10 minutes | Cook time: 7 minutes | Serves 2

- 7 ounces (198 g) mixed greens
- 8 thick slices pork bacon
- 2 shallots, peeled and diced
- Nonstick cooking spray

1. Begin by preheating the Air fryer to 170°C.
2. Now, add the shallot and bacon to the Air fryer cooking basket; set the timer for 2 minutes. Spritz with a nonstick cooking spray.
3. After that, pause the Air fryer; throw in the mixed greens; give it a good stir and cook an additional 5 minutes. Serve warm.

Lamb Loin Chops with Garlic

Prep Time: 8minutes Cooking Time: 30 minutes Servings: 4

- 3 garlic cloves, crushed
- 1 tbsp. fresh lemon juice
- 1 tsp. olive oil
- flake salt and ground black pepper, as required
- 8 (3½-oz.) bone-in lamb loin chops, trimmed

1. In a bowl, mix garlic, lemon juice, oil, salt, and black pepper.
2. Add chops and generously coat with the mixture.
3. Set the temperature of the Air fryer to 200°C and time to 15 minutes.
4. Grease a air fryer basket or wire rack.
5. Arrange chops into the prepared air fryer basket or wire rack in a single layer in 2 batches.
6. Flip once after every 5 minutes per side.
7. Remove from the Air fryer and transfer the chops onto plates.
8. Serve hot.

Roast Pork Tenderloin

Prep time: 20 minutes | Cook time: 17 minutes | Serves 4

- 1 pound (454 g) pork tenderloin
- 4-5 garlic cloves, peeled and halved
- 1 teaspoon flaked salt
- ⅓ teaspoon ground black pepper
- 1 teaspoon dried basil
- ½ teaspoon dried oregano
- ½ teaspoon dried rosemary
- ½ teaspoon dried marjoram
- 2 tablespoons cooking wine

1. Rub the pork with garlic halves; add the seasoning and drizzle with the cooking wine. Then, cut slits completely through pork tenderloin. Tuck the remaining garlic into the slits.
2. Wrap the pork tenderloin with foil; let it marinate overnight.
3. Roast at 180°C for 15 to 17 minutes. Serve warm.

Aromatic Pork Loin Roast

Prep time: 55 minutes | Cook time: 55 minutes | Serves 6

- 1½ pounds (680g) boneless pork loin roast, washed
- 1 teaspoon mustard seeds
- 1 teaspoon garlic powder
- 1 teaspoon porcini powder
- 1 teaspoon shallot powder
- ¾ teaspoon sea salt flakes
- 1 teaspoon red pepper flakes, crushed
- 2 dried sprigs thyme, crushed
- 2 tablespoons lime juice

1. Firstly, score the meat using a small knife; make sure to not cut too deep.
2. In a small-sized mixing dish, combine all seasonings in the order listed above; mix to combine well.
3. Massage the spice mix into the pork meat to evenly distribute. Drizzle with lemon juice.
4. Then, set your Air fryer to cook at 180°C. Place the pork in the air fryer basket or wire rack; roast for 25 to 30 minutes. Pause the machine, check for doneness and cook for 25 minutes more.

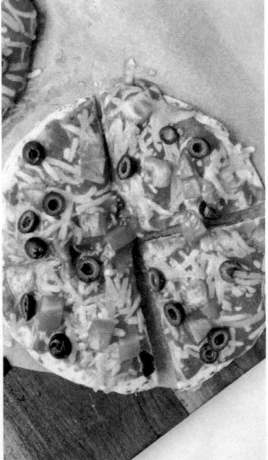

Pork Cheese Casserole

Prep time: 50 minutes | Cook time: 30 minutes | Serves 4

- 2 chili peppers
- 1 red bell pepper
- 2 tablespoons olive oil
- 1 large-sized shallot, chopped
- 1 pound (454 g) ground pork
- 2 garlic cloves, minced
- 2 ripe tomatoes, puréed
- 1 teaspoon dried marjoram
- ½ teaspoon mustard seeds
- ½ teaspoon celery seeds
- 1 teaspoon Mexican oregano
- 1 tablespoon fish sauce
- 2 tablespoons fresh coriander, chopped
- Salt and ground black pepper, to taste
- 2 cups water
- 1 tablespoon chicken bouillon granules
- 2 tablespoons sherry wine
- 1 cup Mexican cheese blend

1. Roast the peppers in the preheated Air fryer at 200°C for 10 minutes, flipping them halfway through cook time.
2. Let them steam for 10 minutes; then, peel the skin and discard the stems and seeds. Slice the peppers into halves.
3. Heat the olive oil in a baking pan at 190°C for 2 minutes; add the shallots and cook for 4 minutes. Add the ground pork and garlic; cook for a further 4 to 5 minutes.
4. After that, stir in the tomatoes, marjoram, mustard seeds, celery seeds, oregano, fish sauce, coriander, salt, and pepper. Add a layer of sliced peppers to the baking pan.
5. Mix the water with the chicken bouillon granules and sherry wine. Add the mixture to the baking pan.
6. Cook in the preheated Air fryer at 200°C for 10 minutes. Top with cheese and bake an additional 5 minutes until the cheese has melted. Serve immediately.

Chapter 5
Fish and Seafood

Honey-Glazed Cod with Sesame Seeds

Prep time: 5 minutes | Cook time: 7 to 9 minutes | Makes 1 fillet

- 1 tablespoon reduced-sodium soy sauce
- 2 teaspoons honey
- Cooking spray
- 6 ounces (170 g) fresh cod fillet
- 1 teaspoon sesame seeds

1. Preheat the air fryer to 180°C .
2. In a small bowl, combine the soy sauce and honey.
3. Spray the baking pan with cooking spray, then place the cod in the pan, brush with the soy mixture, and sprinkle sesame seeds on top. Bake for 7 to 9 minutes or until opaque.
4. Remove the fish and allow to cool on a wire rack for 5 minutes before serving.

Italian-Style Salmon Patties

Prep time: 10 minutes | Cook time: 8 minutes | Serves 4

- 2 (5-ounce / 142 g) cans salmon, flaked
- 2 large eggs, beaten
- ⅓ cup minced onion
- ⅔ cup panko bread crumbs
- 1½ teaspoons Italian-Style seasoning
- 1 teaspoon garlic powder
- Cooking spray

1. In a medium bowl, stir together the salmon, eggs, and onion.
2. In a small bowl, whisk the bread crumbs, Italian-Style seasoning, and garlic powder until blended. Add the bread crumb mixture to the salmon mixture and stir until blended. Shape the mixture into 8 patties.
3. Preheat the air fryer to 180°C. Line the baking pan with greaseproof paper.
4. Working in batches as needed, place the patties on the parchment and spritz with oil.
5. Bake for 4 minutes. Flip, spritz the patties with oil, and bake for 4 to 8 minutes more, until browned and firm. Serve.

Garlic-Lemon Prawn

Prep time: 10 minutes | Cook time: 14 minutes | Serves 4

- 2 teaspoons minced garlic
- 2 teaspoons lemon juice
- 2 teaspoons olive oil
- ½ to 1 teaspoon crushed red pepper
- 12 ounces (340 g) medium Prawn, deveined, with tails on
- Cooking spray

1. In a medium bowl, mix together the garlic, lemon juice, olive oil, and crushed red pepper to make a marinade.
2. Add the Prawn and toss to coat in the marinade. Cover with Cling Film and place the bowl in the refrigerator for 30 minutes.
3. Preheat the air fryer to 200°C. Spray the baking pan lightly with cooking spray.
4. Place the Prawn in the pan. Bake for 6 minutes. Stir and bake until the Prawn are cooked through and nicely browned, an additional 8 minutes. Cool for 5 minutes before serving.

Tuna Casserole with Peppers

Prep time: 10 minutes | Cook time: 16 minutes | Serves 4

- ½ tablespoon sesame oil
- ⅓ cup yellow onions, chopped
- ½ bell pepper, seeded and chopped
- 2 cups tinned tuna, chopped
- Cooking spray
- 5 eggs, beaten
- ½ chili pepper, seeded and finely minced
- 1½ tablespoons Soured cream
- ⅓ teaspoon dried basil
- ⅓ teaspoon dried oregano
- Fine sea salt and ground black pepper, to taste

1. Heat the sesame oil in a nonstick frying pan over medium heat until it shimmers.
2. Add the onions and bell pepper and sauté for 4 minutes, stirring occasionally, or until tender.
3. Add the tinned tuna and keep stirring until the tuna is heated through.
4. Meanwhile, coat a baking dish lightly with cooking spray.
5. Transfer the tuna mixture to the baking dish, along with the beaten eggs, chili pepper, Soured cream, basil, and oregano. Stir to combine well. Season with sea salt and black pepper.
6. Preheat the air fryer to 160°C.
7. Place the baking dish in the air fryer and bake for 12 minutes, or until the top is lightly browned and the eggs are completely set.
8. Remove from the air fryer and serve on a plate.

Baked Bacon-Wrapped Scallops

Prep time: 5 minutes | Cook time: 12 minutes | Serves 4

- 8 slices bacon, cut in half
- 16 sea scallops, patted dry
- Cooking spray
- Salt and freshly ground black pepper, to taste
- 16 Cocktail Sticks, soaked in water for at least 30 minutes

1. Preheat the air fryer to 200°C.
2. On a clean work surface, wrap half of a slice of bacon around each scallop and secure with a toothpick.
3. Lay the bacon-wrapped scallops in the baking pan in a single layer. You may need to work in batches to avoid overcrowding.
4. Spritz the scallops with cooking spray and sprinkle the salt and pepper to season.
5. Bake for 12 minutes, flipping the scallops halfway through, or until the bacon is cooked through and the scallops are firm.
6. Remove the scallops from the air fryer to a plate and repeat with the remaining scallops. Serve warm.

White Fish, Carrot and Cabbage Tacos

Prep time: 10 minutes | Cook time: 15 minutes | Serves 4

- 1 pound (454 g) white fish fillets
- 2 teaspoons olive oil
- 3 tablespoons freshly squeezed lemon juice, divided
- 1½ cups chopped red cabbage
- 1 large carrot, grated
- ½ cup low-sodium salsa
- ⅓ cup low-fat Greek yogurt
- 4 soft low-sodium whole-wheat tortillas

1. Preheat the air fryer to 200°C.
2. Brush the fish with the olive oil and sprinkle with 1 tablespoon of lemon juice. Bake in the baking pan for 15 minutes, or until the fish just flakes when tested with a fork.
3. Meanwhile, in a medium bowl, stir together the remaining 2 tablespoons of lemon juice, the red cabbage, carrot, salsa, and yogurt.
4. When the fish is cooked, remove it from the pan and break it up into large pieces.
5. Offer the fish, tortillas, and the cabbage mixture, and let each person assemble a taco.
6. Serve immediately.

Lemon-Caper Salmon Burgers

Prep time: 15 minutes | Cook time: 15 minutes | Serves 5

- Lemon-Caper Rémoulade:
- ½ cup mayonnaise
- 2 tablespoons minced drained capers
- 2 tablespoons chopped fresh parsley
- 2 teaspoons fresh lemon juice
- Salmon Patties:
- 1 pound (454 g) wild salmon fillet, skinned and pin bones removed
- 6 tablespoons panko bread crumbs
- ¼ cup minced red onion plus ¼ cup slivered for serving
- 1 garlic clove, minced
- 1 large egg, lightly beaten
- 1 tablespoon Dijon mustard
- 1 teaspoon fresh lemon juice
- 1 tablespoon chopped fresh parsley
- ½ teaspoon flaked salt
- For Serving:
- 5 whole wheat potato buns or gluten-free buns
- 10 butter lettuce leaves

1. For the lemon-caper rémoulade: In a small bowl, combine the mayonnaise, capers, parsley, and lemon juice and mix well.
2. For the salmon patties: Cut off a 4-ounce / 113-g piece of the salmon and transfer to a food processor. Pulse until it becomes pasty. With a sharp knife, chop the remaining salmon into small cubes.
3. In a medium bowl, combine the chopped and processed salmon with the panko, minced red onion, garlic, egg, mustard, lemon juice, parsley, and salt. Toss gently to combine. Form the mixture into 5 patties about ¾ inch thick. Refrigerate for at least 30 minutes.
4. Preheat the air fryer to 200°C.
5. Working in batches, place the patties in the baking pan. Bake for about 15 minutes, gently flipping halfway, until golden and cooked through.
6. To serve, transfer each patty to a bun. Top each with 2 lettuce leaves, 2 tablespoons of the rémoulade, and the slivered red onions.

Crab Ratatouille with Tomatoes and aubergine

Prep time: 15 minutes | Cook time: 11 to 14 minutes | Serves 4

- 1½ cups peeled and cubed aubergine
- 2 large tomatoes, chopped
- 1 red bell pepper, chopped
- 1 onion, chopped
- 1 tablespoon olive oil
- ½ teaspoon dried basil
- ½ teaspoon dried thyme
- Pinch salt
- Freshly ground black pepper, to taste
- 1½ cups cooked crab meat

1. Preheat the air fryer to 200°C.
2. In a metal bowl, stir together the aubergine, tomatoes, bell pepper, onion, olive oil, basil and thyme. Season with salt and pepper.
3. Place the bowl in the preheated air fryer and bake for 9 minutes.
4. Remove the bowl from the air fryer. Add the crab meat and stir well and bake for another 2 to 5 minutes, or until the vegetables are softened and the ratatouille is bubbling.
5. Serve warm.

Breaded Calamari Rings with Lemon

Prep time: 5 minutes | Cook time: 12 minutes | Serves 4

- 2 large eggs
- 2 garlic cloves, minced
- ½ cup cornflour
- 1 cup bread crumbs
- 1 pound (454 g) calamari rings
- Cooking spray
- 1 lemon, sliced

1. In a small bowl, whisk the eggs with minced garlic. Place the cornflour and bread crumbs into separate shallow dishes.
2. Dredge the calamari rings in the cornflour, then dip in the egg mixture, shaking off any excess, finally roll them in the bread crumbs to coat well. Let the calamari rings sit for 10 minutes in the refrigerator.
3. Preheat the air fryer to 200°C. Spritz the baking pan with cooking spray.
4. Put the calamari rings in the pan and bake for 15 minutes until cooked through. Stir halfway through the cooking time.
5. Serve the calamari rings with the lemon slices sprinkled on top.

Almond-Lemon Crusted Fish

Prep time: 10 minutes | Cook time: 9 minutes | Serves 4

- ½ cup raw whole almonds
- 1 scallion, finely chopped
- Grated zest and juice of 1 lemon
- ½ tablespoon extra-virgin olive oil
- ¾ teaspoon flaked salt, divided
- Freshly ground black pepper, to taste
- 4 (6 ounces / 170 g each) skinless fish fillets
- Cooking spray
- 1 teaspoon Dijon mustard

1. In a food processor, pulse the almonds to coarsely chop. Transfer to a small bowl and add the scallion, lemon zest, and olive oil. Season with ¼ teaspoon of the salt and pepper to taste and mix to combine.
2. Spray the top of the fish with oil and squeeze the lemon juice over the fish. Season with the remaining ½ teaspoon salt and pepper to taste. Spread the mustard on top of the fish. Dividing evenly, press the almond mixture onto the top of the fillets to adhere.
3. Preheat the air fryer to 200°C.
4. Working in batches, place the fillets in the baking pan in a single layer. Bake for 9 minutes, until the crumbs start to brown and the fish is cooked through.
5. Serve immediately.

Almond-Coconut Flounder Fillets

Prep time: 8 minutes | Cook time: 12 minutes | Serves 2

- 2 flounder fillets, patted dry
- 1 egg
- ½ teaspoon Worcestershire sauce
- ¼ cup almond flour
- ¼ cup coconut flour
- ½ teaspoon coarse sea salt
- ½ teaspoon lemon pepper
- ¼ teaspoon chili powder
- Cooking spray

1. Preheat the air fryer to 200°C. Spritz the baking pan with cooking spray.
2. In a shallow bowl, beat together the egg with Worcestershire sauce until well incorporated.
3. In another bowl, thoroughly combine the almond flour, coconut flour, sea salt, lemon pepper, and chili powder.
4. Dredge the fillets in the egg mixture, shaking off any excess, then roll in the flour mixture to coat well.
5. Place the fillets in the pan and bake for 7 minutes. Flip the fillets and spray with cooking spray. Continue cooking for 5 minutes, or until the fish is flaky.
6. Serve warm.

Old Bay Salmon Patty Bites

Prep time: 15 minutes | Cook time: 15 minutes | Serves 4

- 4 (5-ounce / 142-g) cans pink salmon, skinless, boneless in water, drained
- 2 eggs, beaten
- 1 cup whole-wheat panko bread crumbs
- 4 tablespoons finely minced red bell pepper
- 2 tablespoons parsley flakes
- 2 teaspoons Old Bay seasoning
- Cooking spray

1. Preheat the air fryer to 200°C.
2. Spray the baking pan lightly with cooking spray.
3. In a medium bowl, mix the salmon, eggs, panko bread crumbs, red bell pepper, parsley flakes, and Old Bay seasoning.
4. Using a small biscuit scoop, form the mixture into 20 balls.
5. Place the salmon bites in the pan in a single layer and spray lightly with cooking spray. You may need to cook them in batches.
6. Bake for 15 minutes, stirring a couple of times for even cooking.
7. Serve immediately.

Parmesan Sriracha Tuna Patty Sliders

Prep time: 15 minutes | Cook time: 15 minutes | Serves 4

- 3 (5-ounce / 142-g) cans tuna, packed in water
- ⅔ cup whole-wheat panko bread crumbs
- ⅓ cup shredded Parmesan cheese
- 1 tablespoon sriracha
- ¾ teaspoon black pepper
- 10 whole-wheat slider buns
- Cooking spray

1. Preheat the air fryer to 190°C.
2. Spray the baking pan lightly with cooking spray.
3. In a medium bowl combine the tuna, bread crumbs, Parmesan cheese, sriracha, and black pepper and stir to combine.
4. Form the mixture into 10 patties.
5. Place the patties in the pan in a single layer. Spray the patties lightly with cooking spray. You may need to cook them in batches.
6. Bake for 8 minutes. Turn the patties over and lightly spray with cooking spray. Bake until golden brown and crisp, another 7 more minutes. Serve warm.

Smoked Paprika Salmon in White Wine

Prep time: 5 minutes | Cook time: 12 minutes | Serves 4

- 4 tablespoons butter, melted
- 2 cloves garlic, minced
- Sea salt and ground black pepper, to taste
- ¼ cup dry white wine
- 1 tablespoon lime juice
- 1 teaspoon smoked paprika
- ½ teaspoon onion powder
- 4 salmon steaks
- Cooking spray

1. Place all the ingredients except the salmon and oil in a shallow dish and stir to mix well.
2. Add the salmon steaks, turning to coat well on both sides. Transfer the salmon to the refrigerator to marinate for 30 minutes.
3. Preheat the air fryer to 200°C.
4. Place the salmon steaks in the baking pan, discarding any excess marinade. Spray the salmon steaks with cooking spray.
5. Bake for about 12 minutes, flipping the salmon steaks halfway through, or until cooked to your preferred doneness.
6. Divide the salmon steaks among four plates and serve.

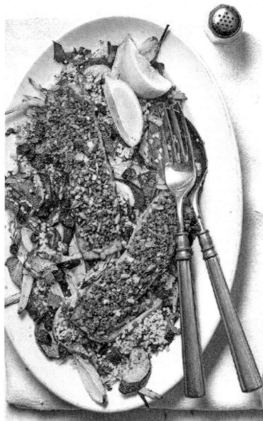

Chapter 6
Vegan and Vegetarian

Ranch Cheddar Cauliflower Steaks
Prep time: 10 minutes | Cook time: 15 minutes | Serves 2

- 1 head cauliflower, stemmed and leaves removed
- ¼ cup rapeseed oil
- ½ teaspoon garlic powder
- ½ teaspoon paprika
- Sea salt, to taste
- Freshly ground black pepper, to taste
- 1 cup shredded Cheddar cheese
- Ranch dressing, for garnish
- 4 slices bacon, cooked and crumbled
- 2 tablespoons chopped fresh chives

1. Cut the cauliflower from top to bottom into two 2-inch "steaks"; reserve the remaining cauliflower to cook separately.
2. Insert the Grill Grate and close the hood. Select GRILL, set the temperature to MAX, and set the time to 15 minutes. Select START/STOP to begin preheating.
3. Meanwhile, in a small bowl, whisk together the oil, garlic powder, and paprika. Season with salt and pepper. Brush each steak with the oil mixture on both sides.
4. When the unit beeps to signify it has preheated, place the steaks on the Grill Grate. Close the hood and cook for 10 minutes.
5. After 10 minutes, flip the steaks and top each with ½ cup of cheese. Close the hood and continue to cook until the cheese is melted, about 5 minutes.
6. When cooking is complete, place the cauliflower steaks on a plate and drizzle with the ranch dressing. Top with the bacon and chives.

Teriyaki Cauliflower
Prep time: 5 minutes | Cook time: 14 minutes | Serves 4

- ½ cup soy sauce
- ⅓ cup water
- 1 tablespoon Demerara sugar
- 1 teaspoon sesame oil
- 1 teaspoon cornflour
- 2 cloves garlic, chopped
- ½ teaspoon chili powder
- 1 big cauliflower head, cut into florets

1. Make the teriyaki sauce: In a small bowl, whisk together the soy sauce, water, Demerara sugar, sesame oil, cornflour, garlic, and chili powder until well combined.
2. Place the cauliflower florets in a large bowl and drizzle the top with the prepared teriyaki sauce and toss to coat well.
3. Put the cauliflower florets in the air fry basket.
4. Select Air Fry, set temperature to 170°C and set time to 14 minutes. Select Start/Stop to begin preheating.
5. Once preheated, place the air fryer basket or wire rack on the air fry position. Stir the cauliflower halfway through.
6. When cooking is complete, the cauliflower should be crisp-tender.
7. Let the cauliflower cool for 5 minutes before serving.

Baked Turnip and Courgette
Prep time: 5 minutes | Cook time: 18 minutes | Serves 4

- 3 turnips, sliced
- 1 large courgette, sliced
- 1 large red onion, cut into rings
- 2 cloves garlic, crushed
- 1 tablespoon olive oil
- Salt and black pepper, to taste

1. Put the turnips, courgette, red onion, and garlic in a baking pan. Drizzle the olive oil over the top and sprinkle with the salt and pepper.
2. Select Bake, set temperature to 170°C, and set time to 18 minutes. Select Start/Stop to begin preheating.
3. Once preheated, place the pan on the bake position.
4. When cooking is complete, the vegetables should be tender. Remove from the oven and serve on a plate.

Fried Root Vegetable Medley with Thyme
Prep time: 10 minutes | Cook time: 22 minutes | Serves 4

- 2 carrots, sliced
- 2 potatoes, cut into chunks
- 1 swede, cut into chunks
- 1 turnip, cut into chunks
- 1 beetroot, cut into chunks
- 8 shallots, halved
- 2 tablespoons olive oil
- Salt and black pepper, to taste
- 2 tablespoons tomato pesto
- 2 tablespoons water
- 2 tablespoons chopped fresh thyme

1. Toss the carrots, potatoes, swede, turnip, beetroot, shallots, olive oil, salt, and pepper in a large mixing bowl until the root vegetables are evenly coated.
2. Place the root vegetables in the air fry basket.
3. Select Air Fry, set temperature to 200°C and set time to 22 minutes. Select Start/Stop to begin preheating.
4. Once preheated, place the air fryer basket or wire rack on the air fry position. Stir the vegetables twice during cooking.
5. When cooking is complete, the vegetables should be tender.
6. Meanwhile, in a small bowl, whisk together the tomato pesto and water until smooth.
7. When ready, remove the root vegetables from the oven to a platter. Drizzle with the tomato pesto mixture and sprinkle with the thyme. Serve immediately.

Vegetable and Cheese Stuffed Tomatoes

Prep time: 10 minutes | Cook time: 18 minutes | Serves 4

- 4 medium beefsteak tomatoes, rinsed
- ½ cup grated carrot
- 1 medium onion, chopped
- 1 garlic clove, minced
- 2 teaspoons olive oil
- 2 cups fresh baby spinach
- ¼ cup crumbled low-sodium feta cheese
- ½ teaspoon dried basil

1. On your cutting board, cut a thin slice off the top of each tomato. Scoop out a ¼- to ½-inch-thick tomato pulp and place the tomatoes upside down on kitchen paper to drain. Set aside.
2. Stir together the carrot, onion, garlic, and olive oil in a baking pan.
3. Select Bake, Super Convection. Set temperature to 180°C and set time to 5 minutes. Select Start/Stop to begin preheating.
4. Once preheated, place the pan on the bake position. Stir the vegetables halfway through.
5. When cooking is complete, the carrot should be crisp-tender.
6. Remove the pan from the oven and stir in the spinach, feta cheese, and basil.
7. Spoon ¼ of the vegetable mixture into each tomato and transfer the stuffed tomatoes to the oven. Set time to 13 minutes.
8. When cooking is complete, the filling should be hot and the tomatoes should be lightly caramelized.
9. Let the tomatoes cool for 5 minutes and serve.

Cashew Cauliflower with Yogurt Sauce

Prep time: 5 minutes | Cook time: 12 minutes | Serves 2

- 4 cups cauliflower florets (about half a large head)
- 1 tablespoon olive oil
- 1 teaspoon curry powder
- Salt, to taste
- ½ cup toasted, chopped cashews, for garnish
- Yogurt Sauce:
- ¼ cup plain yogurt
- 2 tablespoons Soured cream
- 1 teaspoon honey
- 1 teaspoon lemon juice
- Pinch cayenne pepper
- Salt, to taste
- 1 tablespoon chopped fresh Coriander, plus leaves for garnish

1. In a large mixing bowl, toss the cauliflower florets with the olive oil, curry powder, and salt.
2. Place the cauliflower florets in the air fry basket.
3. Select Air Fry, set temperature to 200°C and set time to 12 minutes. Select Start/Stop to begin preheating.
4. Once preheated, place the air fryer basket or wire rack on the air fry position. Stir the cauliflower florets twice during cooking.
5. When cooking is complete, the cauliflower should be golden brown.
6. Meanwhile, mix all the ingredients for the yogurt sauce in a small bowl and whisk to combine.
7. Remove the cauliflower from the oven and drizzle with the yogurt sauce. Scatter the toasted cashews and Coriander on top and serve immediately.

Cheesy Rice and Olives Stuffed Peppers

Prep time: 5 minutes | Cook time: 16 to 17 minutes | Serves 4

- 4 red bell peppers, tops sliced off
- 2 cups cooked rice
- 1 cup crumbled feta cheese
- 1 onion, chopped
- ¼ cup sliced kalamata olives
- ¾ cup tomato sauce
- 1 tablespoon Greek seasoning
- Salt and black pepper, to taste
- 2 tablespoons chopped fresh dill, for serving

1. Microwave the red bell peppers for 1 to 2 minutes until tender.
2. When ready, transfer the red bell peppers to a plate to cool.
3. Mix the cooked rice, feta cheese, onion, kalamata olives, tomato sauce, Greek seasoning, salt, and pepper in a medium bowl and stir until well combined.
4. Divide the rice mixture among the red bell peppers and transfer to a greased baking dish.
5. Select Bake, set temperature to 180°C and set time to 15 minutes. Select Start/Stop to begin preheating.
6. Once preheated, place the baking dish on the bake position.
7. When cooking is complete, the rice should be heated through and the vegetables should be soft.
8. Remove from the oven and serve with the dill sprinkled on top.

Rosemary beetroots with Balsamic Glaze

Prep time: 5 minutes | Cook time: 10 minutes | Serves 2

- beetroot:
- 2 beetroots, cubed
- 2 tablespoons olive oil
- 2 springs rosemary, chopped
- Salt and black pepper, to taste
- Balsamic Glaze:
- ⅓ cup balsamic vinegar
- 1 tablespoon honey

1. Combine the beetroots, olive oil, rosemary, salt, and pepper in a mixing bowl and toss until the beetroots are completely coated.
2. Place the beetroots in the air fry basket.
3. Select Air Fry, Super Convection. Set temperature to 200°C and set time to 10 minutes. Select Start/Stop to begin preheating.
4. Once preheated, place the air fryer basket or wire rack on the air fry position. Stir the vegetables halfway through.
5. When cooking is complete, the beetroots should be crisp and browned at the edges.
6. Meanwhile, make the balsamic glaze: Place the balsamic vinegar and honey in a small saucepan and bring to a boil over medium heat. When the sauce boils, reduce the heat to medium-low heat and simmer until the liquid is reduced by half.
7. When ready, remove the beetroots from the oven to a platter. Pour the balsamic glaze over the top and serve immediately.

Easy Cheesy Vegetable Quesadilla

Prep time: 5 minutes | Cook time: 10 minutes | Serves 1

- 1 teaspoon olive oil
- 2 flour tortillas
- ¼ courgette, sliced
- ¼ yellow bell pepper, sliced
- ¼ cup shredded gouda cheese
- 1 tablespoon chopped Coriander
- ½ green onion, sliced

1. Coat the air fry basket with 1 teaspoon of olive oil.
2. Arrange a flour tortilla in the air fry basket and scatter the top with courgette, bell pepper, gouda cheese, Coriander, and green onion. Place the other flour tortilla on top.
3. Select Air Fry, set temperature to 200°C, and set time to 10 minutes. Select Start/Stop to begin preheating.
4. Once preheated, place the air fryer basket or wire rack on the air fry position.
5. When cooking is complete, the tortillas should be lightly browned and the vegetables should be tender. Remove from the oven and cool for 5 minutes before slicing into wedges.

Crispy Fried Okra with Chili

Prep time: 5 minutes | Cook time: 10 minutes | Serves 4

- 3 tablespoons Soured cream
- 2 tablespoons flour
- 2 tablespoons semolina
- ½ teaspoon red chili powder
- Salt and black pepper, to taste
- 1 pound (454 g) okra, halved
- Cooking spray

1. Spray the air fry basket with cooking spray. Set aside.
2. In a shallow bowl, place the Soured cream. In another shallow bowl, thoroughly combine the flour, semolina, red chili powder, salt, and pepper.
3. Dredge the okra in the Soured cream, then roll in the flour mixture until evenly coated. Transfer the okra to the air fry basket.
4. Select Air Fry, set temperature to 200°C, and set time to 10 minutes. Select Start/Stop to begin preheating.
5. Once preheated, place the air fryer basket or wire rack on the air fry position. Flip the okra halfway through the cooking time.
6. When cooking is complete, the okra should be golden brown and crispy. Remove the air fryer basket or wire rack from the oven. Cool for 5 minutes before serving.

Crispy Veggies with Halloumi

Prep time: 5 minutes | Cook time: 14 minutes | Serves 2

- 2 courgettes, cut into even chunks
- 1 large aubergine, peeled, cut into chunks
- 1 large carrot, cut into chunks
- 6 ounces (170 g) halloumi cheese, cubed
- 2 teaspoons olive oil
- Salt and black pepper, to taste
- 1 teaspoon dried mixed herbs

1. Combine the courgettes, aubergine, carrot, cheese, olive oil, salt, and pepper in a large bowl and toss to coat well.
2. Spread the mixture evenly in the air fry basket.
3. Select Air Fry, set temperature to 170°C, and set time to 14 minutes. Select Start/Stop to begin preheating.
4. Once preheated, place the air fryer basket or wire rack on the air fry position. Stir the mixture once during cooking.
5. When cooking is complete, they should be crispy and golden. Remove from the oven and serve topped with mixed herbs.

Banana-Choco Brownies

Prep Time: 6 minutes |Cooking Time: 30 minutes| Servings: 12

- 2 cups almond flour
- 3 tsp. Baking powder
- ½ tsp. salt
- 1 over-ripe banana
- 3 large eggs
- ½ tsp. stevia powder
- ¼ cup coconut oil
- 1 tbsp. vinegar
- 1/3 cup almond flour
- 1/3 cup cocoa powder

1. Preheat the Air fryer for 5 minutes.
2. Pulse all the listed ingredients in a food processor until well-combined.
3. Pour the batter into a baking tin will fit in the Air fryer.
4. Place in the air fryer basket or wire rack and set the temperature to 160°C, and time to 30 minutes.
5. If a toothpick inserted in the middle, it should come out clean.

Chocolate Butter Cake

Prep time: 20 minutes | Cook time: 11 minutes | Serves 4

- 4 ounces (113 g) butter, melted
- 4 ounces (113 g) dark chocolate
- 2 eggs, lightly whisked
- 2 tablespoons monk fruit
- 2 tablespoons almond meal
- 1 teaspoon baking powder
- ½ teaspoon ground cinnamon
- ¼ teaspoon ground star anise

1. Begin by preheating your Air fryer to 190°C. Spritz the sides and bottom of a baking pan with nonstick cooking spray.
2. Melt the butter and dark chocolate in a microwave-safe bowl. Mix the eggs and monk fruit until frothy.
3. Pour the butter/chocolate mixture into the egg mixture. Stir in the almond meal, baking powder, cinnamon, and star anise. Mix until everything is well incorporated.
4. Scrape the batter into the prepared pan. Bake in the preheated Air fryer for 9 to 11 minutes.
5. Let stand for 2 minutes. Invert on a plate while warm and serve. Bon appétit!

Cherry-Choco Bars

Prep Time: 8 minutes |Cooking Time: 15 minutes| Servings: 8

- ¼ tsp. salt
- ½ cup almonds, sliced
- ½ cup chia seeds
- ½ cup dark chocolate, chopped
- ½ cup dried cherries, chopped
- ½ cup prunes, pureed
- ½ cup quinoa, cooked
- ¾ cup almond butter
- 1/3 cup honey
- 2 cups old-fashioned oats
- 2 tbsp. coconut oil

1. Preheat the Air fryer to 190°C for 5 minutes.
2. In a bowl, combine the oats, quinoa, chia seeds, almond, cherries, and chocolate.
3. In a saucepan, heat the almond butter, honey, and coconut oil.
4. Pour the butter mixture over the oat mix. Add salt and prunes.
5. Mix until well combined.
6. Pour over a baking dish that can fit inside the Air fryer.
7. Cook for 15 minutes.
8. Let it cool before slicing into bars.

Creamy Cheese Cake

Prep time: 1 hour | Cook time: 37 minutes | Serves 8

1½ cups almond flour
3 ounces (85 g) Swerve
½ stick butter, melted
20 ounces (567 g) full-fat cream cheese
½ cup double cream
1¼ cups granulated Swerve
3 eggs, at room temperature
1 tablespoon vanilla essence
1 teaspoon grated lemon zest

1. Coat the sides and bottom of a baking pan with a little flour.
2. In a mixing bowl, combine the almond flour and Swerve. Add the melted butter and mix until your mixture looks like bread crumbs.
3. Press the mixture into the bottom of the prepared pan to form an even layer. Bake at 170°C for 7 minutes until golden brown. Allow it to cool completely on a wire rack.
4. Meanwhile, in a mixer fitted with the paddle attachment, prepare the filling by mixing the soft cheese, double cream, and granulated Swerve; beat until creamy and fluffy.
5. Crack the eggs into the mixing bowl, one at a time; add the vanilla and lemon zest and continue to mix until fully combined.
6. Pour the prepared topping over the cooled crust and spread evenly.
7. Bake in the preheated Air fryer at 170°C for 25 to 30 minutes; leave it in the Air fryer to keep warm for another 30 minutes.
8. Cover your cheesecake with Cling Film. Place in your refrigerator and allow it to cool at least 6 hours or overnight. Serve well chilled.

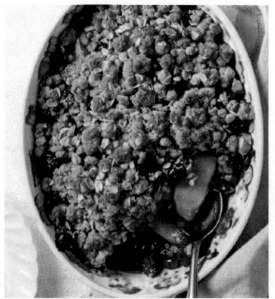

Classic Chocolate Butter Cake
Prep time: 30 minutes | Cook time: 22 minutes | Serves 10

- 1 cup no-sugar-added peanut butter
- 1¼ cups monk fruit
- 3 eggs
- 1 cup almond flour
- 1 teaspoon baking powder
- ¼ teaspoon flake salt
- 1 cup unsweetened chocolate, broken into chunks

1. Start by preheating your Air fryer to 180°C. Now, spritz the sides and bottom of a baking pan with cooking spray.
2. In a mixing dish, thoroughly combine the peanut butter with the monk fruit until creamy. Next, fold in the egg and beat until fluffy.
3. After that, stir in the almond flour, baking powder, salt, and chocolate. Mix until everything is well combined.
4. Bake in the preheated Air fryer for 20 to 22 minutes. Transfer to a wire rack to cool before slicing and serving. Bon appétit!

Buttery Chocolate Cake
Prep time: 20 minutes | Cook time: 11 minutes | Serves 4

- 2½ ounces (71 g) butter, at room temperature
- 3 ounces (85 g) chocolate, unsweetened
- 2 eggs, beaten
- ½ cup Swerve
- ½ cup almond flour
- 1 teaspoon rum extract
- 1 teaspoon vanilla extract

1. Begin by preheating your Air fryer to 190°C. Spritz the sides and bottom of four ramekins with cooking spray.
2. Melt the butter and chocolate in a microwave-safe bowl. Mix the eggs and Swerve until frothy.
3. Pour the butter/chocolate mixture into the egg mixture. Stir in the almond flour, rum extract, and vanilla extract. Mix until everything is well incorporated.
4. Scrape the batter into the prepared ramekins. Bake in the preheated Air fryer for 9 to 11 minutes.
5. Let stand for 2 to 3 minutes. Invert on a plate while warm and serve. Bon appétit!

Butter Chocolate Cake with Pecan

Prep time: 30 minutes | Cook time: 22 minutes | Serves 6

- ½ cup butter, melted
- ½ cup Swerve
- 1 teaspoon vanilla essence
- 1 egg
- ½ cup almond flour
- ½ teaspoon baking powder
- ¼ cup cocoa powder
- ½ teaspoon ground cinnamon
- ¼ teaspoon fine sea salt
- 1 ounce (28 g) chocolate, unsweetened
- ¼ cup pecans, finely chopped

1. Start by preheating your Air fryer to 180°C. Now, lightly grease six silicone molds.
2. In a mixing dish, beat the melted butter with the Swerve until fluffy. Next, stir in the vanilla and egg and beat again.
3. After that, add the almond flour, baking powder, cocoa powder, cinnamon, and salt. Mix until everything is well combined.
4. Fold in the chocolate and pecans; mix to combine. Bake in the preheated Air fryer for 20 to 22 minutes. Enjoy!

Air Fried Chocolate Brownies

Prep time: 40 minutes | Cook time: 35 minutes | Serves 8

- 5 ounces (142 g) unsweetened chocolate, chopped into chunks
- 2 tablespoons instant espresso powder
- 1 tablespoon cocoa powder, unsweetened
- ½ cup almond butter
- ½ cup almond meal
- ¾ cup Swerve
- 1 teaspoon pure coffee extract
- ½ teaspoon lime peel zest
- ¼ cup coconut flour
- 2 eggs plus 1 egg yolk
- ½ teaspoon baking soda
- ½ teaspoon baking powder
- ½ teaspoon ground cinnamon
- ⅓ teaspoon ancho chile powder
- For the Chocolate Mascarpone Frosting:
- 4 ounces (113 g) mascarpone cheese, at room temperature
- 1½ ounces (43 g) unsweetened chocolate chips
- 1½ cups Swerve
- ¼ cup unsalted butter, at room temperature
- 1 teaspoon vanilla paste
- A pinch of fine sea salt

1. First of all, microwave the chocolate and almond butter until completely melted; allow the mixture to cool at room temperature.
2. Then, whisk the eggs, Swerve, cinnamon, espresso powder, coffee extract, ancho chile powder, and lime zest.
3. Next step, add the vanilla/egg mixture to the chocolate/butter mixture. Stir in the almond meal and coconut flour along with baking soda, baking powder and cocoa powder.
4. Finally, press the batter into a lightly buttered cake pan. Air-fry for 35 minutes at 170°C.
5. In the meantime, make the frosting. Beat the butter and mascarpone cheese until creamy. Add in the melted chocolate chips and vanilla paste.
6. Gradually, stir in the Swerve and salt; beat until everything's well combined. Lastly, frost the brownies and serve.

Crispy Peaches

Prep Time: 6 minutes |Cooking Time: 30 minutes |Servings: 4

- 1 tsp. cinnamon
- 3 tsp. sugar, white
- 1/3 cup oats, dry rolled
- 1/4 cup Flour, white
- 2 tbsp. Flour, white
- 3 tbsp. butter, unsalted
- 3 tbsp. sugar
- 3 tbsp. pecans, chopped
- 4 cups sliced peaches, frozen

1. Lightly grease baking pan of the Air fryer with cooking spray.
2. Mix in cinnamon, 2 tbsp flour, sugar, and peaches
3. For 20 minutes, cook on 150°C
4. Mix the other ingredients in a bowl and pour over peaches.
5. Cook for 10 minutes at 170°C
6. Serve and enjoy.

Blueberry Apple Crumble

Prep Time: 7 minutes| Cooking Time: 15 minutes |Servings: 2

- 2 ramekins
- 1 red apple
- 1/2 cup frozen blueberries
- 1/4 cup plus
- 1 tbsp. brown ground rice
- 2 tbsp. sugar
- 1/2 tsp. ground cinnamon
- 2 tbsp. butter

1. Finely dice the red apples.
2. Mix the fruit in one bowl and all other ingredients in another.
3. Preheat the Air fryer to 160°C for 5 minutes
4. Put the fruit in ramekins and sprinkle the flour mixture over it.
5. Bake in the fryer for 15 minutes

Buttery biscuit with Hazelnut

Prep time: 20 minutes | Cook time: 10 minutes | Serves 6

- 1 cup almond flour
- ½ cup coconut flour
- 1 teaspoon baking soda
- 1 teaspoon fine sea salt
- 1 stick butter
- 1 cup Swerve
- 2 teaspoons vanilla
- 2 eggs, at room temperature
- 1 cup hazelnuts, coarsely chopped

1. Begin by preheating your Air fryer to 180°C.
2. Mix the flour with the baking soda, and sea salt.
3. In the bowl of an electric mixer, beat the butter, Swerve, and vanilla until creamy. Fold in the eggs, one at a time, and mix until well combined.
4. Slowly and gradually, stir in the flour mixture. Finally, fold in the coarsely chopped hazelnuts.
5. Divide the dough into small balls using a large biscuit scoop; drop onto the prepared biscuit sheets. Bake for 10 minutes or until golden brown, rotating the pan once or twice through the cooking time.
6. Work in batches and cool for a couple of minutes before removing to wire racks. Enjoy!

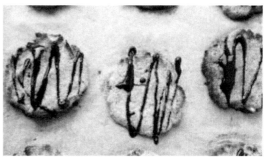

Chapter 8
Fast and Easy Everyday Favourites

Buttered Knots with Parsley

Prep time: 5 minutes | Cook time: 5 minutes | Makes 8 knots

- 1 teaspoon dried parsley
- ¼ cup melted butter
- 2 teaspoons garlic powder
- 1 (11-ounce / 312-g) tube refrigerated French bread dough, cut into 8 slices

1. Combine the parsley, butter, and garlic powder in a bowl. Stir to mix well.
2. Place the French bread dough slices on a clean work surface, then roll each slice into a 6-inch long rope. Tie the ropes into knots and arrange them on a plate.
3. Transfer the knots into a baking pan. Brush the knots with butter mixture.
4. Select Air Fry, set temperature to 180°C and set time to 5 minutes. Select Start/Stop to begin preheating.
5. Once the oven has preheated, slide the pan into the oven. Flip the knots halfway through the cooking time.
6. When done, the knots should be golden brown. Remove the pan from the oven.
7. Serve immediately.

Okra Chips

Prep time: 5 minutes | Cook time: 16 minutes | Serves 6

- 2 pounds (907 g) fresh okra pods, cut into 1-inch pieces
- 2 tablespoons rapeseed oil
- 1 teaspoon coarse sea salt

1. Stir the oil and salt in a bowl to mix well. Add the okra and toss to coat well. Place the okra in the air fry basket.
2. Select Air Fry, set temperature to 200°C and set time to 16 minutes. Select Start/Stop to begin preheating.
3. Once the oven has preheated, place the air fryer basket or wire rack on the air fry position. Flip the okra at least three times during cooking.
4. When cooked, the okra should be lightly browned. Remove from the oven.
5. Serve immediately.

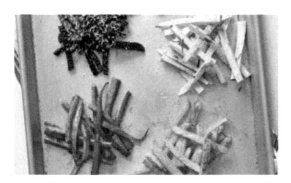

Baked Runner Beans

Prep time: 5 minutes | Cook time: 10 minutes | Makes 2 cups

- ½ teaspoon lemon pepper
- 2 teaspoons granulated garlic
- ½ teaspoon salt
- 1 tablespoon olive oil
- 2 cups fresh Runner Beans, trimmed and snapped in half

1. Combine the lemon pepper, garlic, salt, and olive oil in a bowl. Stir to mix well.
2. Add the Runner Beans to the bowl of mixture and toss to coat well.
3. Arrange the Runner Beans in the air fry basket.
4. Select Bake, set temperature to 190°C and set time to 10 minutes. Select Start/Stop to begin preheating.
5. Once preheated, place the air fryer basket or wire rack on the bake position. Stir the Runner Beans halfway through the cooking time.
6. When cooking is complete, the Runner Beans will be tender and crispy. Remove from the oven.
7. Serve immediately.

Salmon Fillet and Carrot Croquettes

Prep time: 15 minutes | Cook time: 10 minutes | Serves 6

- 2 egg whites
- 1 cup almond flour
- 1 cup panko bread crumbs
- 1 pound (454 g) chopped salmon fillet
- ⅔ cup grated carrots
- 2 tablespoons minced garlic cloves
- ½ cup chopped onion
- 2 tablespoons chopped chives
- Cooking spray

1. Spritz the air fry basket with cooking spray.
2. Whisk the egg whites in a bowl. Put the flour in a second bowl. Pour the bread crumbs in a third bowl. Set aside.
3. Combine the salmon, carrots, garlic, onion, and chives in a large bowl. Stir to mix well.
4. Form the mixture into balls with your hands. Dredge the balls into the flour, then egg, and then bread crumbs to coat well.
5. Arrange the salmon balls in the air fry basket and spritz with cooking spray.
6. Select Air Fry, set temperature to 180°C and set time to 10 minutes. Select Start/Stop to begin preheating.
7. Once preheated, place the air fryer basket or wire rack on the air fry position. Flip the salmon balls halfway through cooking.
8. When cooking is complete, the salmon balls will be crispy and browned. Remove the air fryer basket or wire rack from the oven.
9. Serve immediately.

Kale Chips

Prep time: 5 minutes | Cook time: 5 minutes | Serves 2

- 4 medium kale leaves, about 1 ounce (28 g) each, stems removed, tear the leaves in thirds
- 2 teaspoons soy sauce
- 2 teaspoons olive oil

1. Toss the kale leaves with soy sauce and olive oil in a large bowl to coat well. Place the leaves in the baking pan.
2. Select Air Fry, set temperature to 200°C and set time to 5 minutes. Select Start/Stop to begin preheating.
3. Once the oven has preheated, slide the pan into the oven. Flip the leaves with tongs gently halfway through.
4. When cooked, the kale leaves should be crispy. Remove the pan from the oven.
5. Serve immediately.

Apple Fritters with Sweet Glaze

Prep time: 10 minutes | Cook time: 8 minutes | Makes 15 fritters

- Apple Fritters:
- 2 firm apples, peeled, cored, and diced
- ½ teaspoon cinnamon
- Juice of 1 lemon
- 1 cup plain flour
- 1½ teaspoons baking powder
- ½ teaspoon flaked salt
- 2 eggs
- ¼ cup milk
- 2 tablespoons unsalted butter, melted
- Cooking spray
- Glaze:
- ½ teaspoon vanilla extract
- 1¼ cups icing sugar, sifted
- ¼ cup water

1. Line the air fry basket with greaseproof paper.
2. Combine the apples with cinnamon and lemon juice in a small bowl. Toss to coat well.
3. Combine the flour, baking powder, and salt in a large bowl. Stir to mix well.
4. Whisk the egg, milk, butter, and sugar in a medium bowl. Stir to mix well.
5. Make a well in the center of the flour mixture, then pour the egg mixture into the well and stir to mix well. Mix in the apple until a dough forms.
6. Use an ice cream scoop to scoop 15 balls from the dough onto the pan. Spritz with cooking spray.
7. Select Air Fry, set temperature to 180°C and set time to 8 minutes. Select Start/Stop to begin preheating.
8. Once the oven has preheated, place the air fryer basket or wire rack on the air fry position. Flip the apple fritters halfway through the cooking time.
9. Meanwhile, combine the ingredients for the glaze in a separate small bowl. Stir to mix well.
10. When cooking is complete, the apple fritters will be golden brown. Serve the fritters with the glaze on top or use the glaze for dipping.

Garlicky courgette and Summer marrow

Prep time: 10 minutes | Cook time: 10 minutes | Serves 4

- 2 large courgette, peeled and spiralized
- 2 large yellow summer marrow, peeled and spiralized
- 1 tablespoon olive oil, divided
- ½ teaspoon flaked salt
- 1 garlic clove, whole
- 2 tablespoons fresh basil, chopped
- Cooking spray

1. Spritz the air fry basket with cooking spray.
2. Combine the courgette and summer marrow with 1 teaspoon of the olive oil and salt in a large bowl. Toss to coat well.
3. Transfer the courgette and summer marrow to the air fry basket and add the garlic.
4. Select Air Fry, set temperature to 180°C and set time to 10 minutes. Select Start/Stop to begin preheating.
5. Once preheated, place the air fryer basket or wire rack on the air fry position. Stir the courgette and summer marrow halfway through the cooking time.
6. When cooked, the courgette and summer marrow will be tender and fragrant. Transfer the cooked courgette and summer marrow onto a plate and set aside.
7. Remove the garlic from the oven and allow to cool for 5 minutes. Mince the garlic and combine with remaining olive oil in a small bowl. Stir to mix well.
8. Drizzle the spiralized courgette and summer marrow with garlic oil and sprinkle with basil. Toss to serve.

Roasted Carrot Chips

Prep time: 5 minutes | Cook time: 15 minutes | Makes 3 cups

- 3 large carrots, peeled and sliced into long and thick chips diagonally
- 1 tablespoon granulated garlic
- 1 teaspoon salt
- ¼ teaspoon ground black pepper
- 1 tablespoon olive oil
- 1 tablespoon finely chopped fresh parsley

1. Toss the carrots with garlic, salt, ground black pepper, and olive oil in a large bowl to coat well. Place the carrots in the air fry basket.
2. Select Roast, set temperature to 180°C and set time to 15 minutes. Select Start/Stop to begin preheating.
3. Once the oven has preheated, place the air fryer basket or wire rack on the roast position. Stir the carrots halfway through the cooking time.
4. When cooking is complete, the carrot chips should be soft. Remove from the oven.
5. Serve the carrot chips with parsley on top.

Pears with Lemony Ricotta
Prep time: 10 minutes | Cook time: 8 minutes | Serves 4

- 2 large Bartlett pears, peeled, cut in half, cored
- 3 tablespoons melted butter
- ½ teaspoon ground ginger
- ¼ teaspoon ground cardamom
- 3 tablespoons Demerara sugar
- ½ cup whole-milk ricotta cheese
- 1 teaspoon pure lemon extract
- 1 teaspoon pure almond extract
- 1 tablespoon honey, plus additional for drizzling

1. Toss the pears with butter, ginger, cardamom, and sugar in a large bowl. Toss to coat well. Arrange the pears in a baking pan, cut side down.
2. Select Air Fry, set temperature to 190°C and set time to 8 minutes. Select Start/Stop to begin preheating.
3. Once preheated, place the pan into the oven.
4. After 5 minutes, remove the pan and flip the pears. Return the pan to the oven and continue cooking.
5. When cooking is complete, the pears should be soft and browned. Remove the pan from the oven.
6. In the meantime, combine the remaining ingredients in a separate bowl. Whip for 1 minute with a hand mixer until the mixture is puffed.
7. Divide the mixture into four bowls, then put the pears over the mixture and drizzle with more honey to serve.

Lemony Asparagus
Prep time: 5 minutes | Cook time: 10 minutes | Makes 10 spears

- 10 spears asparagus (about ½ pound / 227 g in total), snap the ends off
- 1 tablespoon lemon juice
- 2 teaspoons minced garlic
- ½ teaspoon salt
- ¼ teaspoon ground black pepper
- Cooking spray

1. Line the air fry basket with greaseproof paper.
2. Put the asparagus spears in a large bowl. Drizzle with lemon juice and sprinkle with minced garlic, salt, and ground black pepper. Toss to coat well.
3. Transfer the asparagus to the air fry basket and spritz with cooking spray.
4. Select Air Fry, set temperature to 200°C and set time to 10 minutes. Select Start/Stop to begin preheating.
5. Once the oven has preheated, place the air fryer basket or wire rack on the air fry position. Flip the asparagus halfway through cooking.
6. When cooked, the asparagus should be wilted and soft. Remove the air fryer basket or wire rack from the oven.
7. Serve immediately.

Old Bay Prawn

Prep time: 10 minutes | Cook time: 10 minutes | Makes 2 cups

- ½ teaspoon Old Bay Seasoning
- 1 teaspoon ground cayenne pepper
- ½ teaspoon paprika
- 1 tablespoon olive oil
- ⅛ teaspoon salt
- ½ pound (227 g) Prawns, peeled and deveined
- Juice of half a lemon

1. Combine the Old Bay Seasoning, cayenne pepper, paprika, olive oil, and salt in a large bowl, then add the Prawns and toss to coat well.
2. Put the Prawns in the air fry basket.
3. Select Air Fry, set temperature to 200°C and set time to 10 minutes. Select Start/Stop to begin preheating.
4. Once preheated, place the air fryer basket or wire rack on the air fry position. Flip the Prawns halfway through the cooking time.
5. When cooking is complete, the Prawns should be opaque. Remove from the oven.
6. Serve the Prawns with lemon juice on top.

Spicy Air Fried Old Bay Prawn

Prep time: 10 minutes | Cook time: 10 minutes | Makes 2 cups

- ½ teaspoon Old Bay Seasoning
- 1 teaspoon ground cayenne pepper
- ½ teaspoon paprika
- 1 tablespoon olive oil
- ⅛ teaspoon salt
- ½ pound (227 g) Prawns, peeled and deveined
- Juice of half a lemon

1. Combine the Old Bay Seasoning, cayenne pepper, paprika, olive oil, and salt in a large bowl, then add the Prawns and toss to coat well.
2. Put the Prawns in the air fry basket.
3. Select Air Fry, set temperature to 200°C and set time to 10 minutes. Select Start/Stop to begin preheating.
4. Once preheated, place the air fryer basket or wire rack on the air fry position. Flip the Prawns halfway through the cooking time.
5. When cooking is complete, the Prawns should be opaque. Remove from the oven.
6. Serve the Prawns with lemon juice on top.

Sweet-Sour Peanut

Prep time: 5 minutes | Cook time: 5 minutes | Serves 9

- 3 cups shelled raw peanuts
- 1 tablespoon hot red pepper sauce
- 3 tablespoons granulated white sugar

1. Put the peanuts in a large bowl, then drizzle with hot red pepper sauce and sprinkle with sugar. Toss to coat well.
2. Pour the peanuts in the air fry basket.
3. Select Air Fry, set temperature to 200°C and set time to 5 minutes. Select Start/Stop to begin preheating.
4. Once preheated, place the air fryer basket or wire rack on the air fry position. Stir the peanuts halfway through the cooking time.
5. When cooking is complete, the peanuts will be crispy and browned. Remove from the oven.
6. Serve immediately.

Carrot Chips

Prep time: 5 minutes | Cook time: 15 minutes | Makes 3 cups

- 3 large carrots, peeled and sliced into long and thick chips diagonally
- 1 tablespoon granulated garlic
- 1 teaspoon salt
- ¼ teaspoon ground black pepper
- 1 tablespoon olive oil
- 1 tablespoon finely chopped fresh parsley

1. Toss the carrots with garlic, salt, ground black pepper, and olive oil in a large bowl to coat well. Place the carrots in the air fry basket.
2. Select Roast, set temperature to 180°C and set time to 15 minutes. Select Start/Stop to begin preheating.
3. Once the oven has preheated, place the air fryer basket or wire rack on the roast position. Stir the carrots halfway through the cooking time.
4. When cooking is complete, the carrot chips should be soft. Remove from the oven.
5. Serve the carrot chips with parsley on top.

Bartlett Pears with Lemony Ricotta

Prep time: 10 minutes | Cook time: 8 minutes | Serves 4

- 2 large Bartlett pears, peeled, cut in half, cored
- 3 tablespoons melted butter
- ½ teaspoon ground ginger
- ¼ teaspoon ground cardamom
- 3 tablespoons Demerara sugar
- ½ cup whole-milk ricotta cheese
- 1 teaspoon pure lemon extract
- 1 teaspoon pure almond extract
- 1 tablespoon honey, plus additional for drizzling

1. Toss the pears with butter, ginger, cardamom, and sugar in a large bowl. Toss to coat well. Arrange the pears in a baking pan, cut side down.
2. Select Air Fry, set temperature to 190°C and set time to 8 minutes. Select Start/Stop to begin preheating.
3. Once preheated, place the pan into the oven.
4. After 5 minutes, remove the pan and flip the pears. Return the pan to the oven and continue cooking.
5. When cooking is complete, the pears should be soft and browned. Remove the pan from the oven.
6. In the meantime, combine the remaining ingredients in a separate bowl. Whip for 1 minute with a hand mixer until the mixture is puffed.
7. Divide the mixture into four bowls, then put the pears over the mixture and drizzle with more honey to serve.

Lemony and Garlicky Asparagus

Prep time: 5 minutes | Cook time: 10 minutes | Makes 10 spears

- 10 spears asparagus (about ½ pound / 227 g in total), snap the ends off
- 1 tablespoon lemon juice
- 2 teaspoons minced garlic
- ½ teaspoon salt
- ¼ teaspoon ground black pepper
- Cooking spray

1. Line the air fry basket with greaseproof paper.
2. Put the asparagus spears in a large bowl. Drizzle with lemon juice and sprinkle with minced garlic, salt, and ground black pepper. Toss to coat well.
3. Transfer the asparagus to the air fry basket and spritz with cooking spray.
4. Select Air Fry, set temperature to 200°C and set time to 10 minutes. Select Start/Stop to begin preheating.
5. Once the oven has preheated, place the air fryer basket or wire rack on the air fry position. Flip the asparagus halfway through cooking.
6. When cooked, the asparagus should be wilted and soft. Remove the air fryer basket or wire rack from the oven.
7. Serve immediately.

Sweet and Sour Peanuts

Prep time: 5 minutes | Cook time: 5 minutes | Serves 9

- 3 cups shelled raw peanuts
- 1 tablespoon hot red pepper sauce
- 3 tablespoons granulated white sugar

1. Put the peanuts in a large bowl, then drizzle with hot red pepper sauce and sprinkle with sugar. Toss to coat well.
2. Pour the peanuts in the air fry basket.
3. Select Air Fry, set temperature to 200°C and set time to 5 minutes. Select Start/Stop to begin preheating.
4. Once preheated, place the air fryer basket or wire rack on the air fry position. Stir the peanuts halfway through the cooking time.
5. When cooking is complete, the peanuts will be crispy and browned. Remove from the oven.
6. Serve immediately.

Appendix 1 Measurement Conversion Chart

Volume Equivalents (Dry)	
US STANDARD	METRIC (APPROXIMATE)
1/8 teaspoon	0.5 mL
1/4 teaspoon	1 mL
1/2 teaspoon	2 mL
3/4 teaspoon	4 mL
1 teaspoon	5 mL
1 tablespoon	15 mL
1/4 cup	59 mL
1/2 cup	118 mL
3/4 cup	177 mL
1 cup	235 mL
2 cups	475 mL
3 cups	700 mL
4 cups	1 L

Volume Equivalents (Liquid)		
US STANDARD	US STANDARD (OUNCES)	METRIC (APPROXIMATE)
2 tablespoons	1 fl.oz.	30 mL
1/4 cup	2 fl.oz.	60 mL
1/2 cup	4 fl.oz.	120 mL
1 cup	8 fl.oz.	240 mL
1 1/2 cup	12 fl.oz.	355 mL
2 cups or 1 pint	16 fl.oz.	475 mL
4 cups or 1 quart	32 fl.oz.	1 L
1 gallon	128 fl.oz.	4 L

Temperatures Equivalents	
FAHRENHEIT(F)	CELSIUS(C) APPROXIMATE)
225 °F	107 °C
250 °F	120 ° °C
275 °F	135 °C
300 °F	150 °C
325 °F	160 °C
350 °F	180 °C
375 °F	190 °C
400 °F	205 °C
425 °F	220 °C
450 °F	235 °C
475 °F	245 °C
500 °F	260 °C

Weight Equivalents	
US STANDARD	METRIC (APPROXIMATE)
1 ounce	28 g
2 ounces	57 g
5 ounces	142 g
10 ounces	284 g
15 ounces	425 g
16 ounces (1 pound)	455 g
1.5 pounds	680 g
2 pounds	907 g

Appendix 2 The Dirty Dozen and Clean Fifteen

The Environmental Working Group (EWG) is a nonprofit, nonpartisan organization dedicated to protecting human health and the environment Its mission is to empower people to live healthier lives in a healthier environment. This organization publishes an annual list of the twelve kinds of produce, in sequence, that have the highest amount of pesticide residue-the Dirty Dozen-as well as a list of the fifteen kinds of produce that have the least amount of pesticide residue-the Clean Fifteen.

THE DIRTY DOZEN	
The 2016 Dirty Dozen includes the following produce. These are considered among the year's most important produce to buy organic:	
Strawberries	Spinach
Apples	Tomatoes
Nectarines	Bell peppers
Peaches	Cherry tomatoes
Celery	Cucumbers
Grapes	Kale/collard greens
Cherries	Hot peppers

The Dirty Dozen list contains two additional itemskale/collard greens and hot peppers-because they tend to contain trace levels of highly hazardous pesticides.

THE CLEAN FIFTEEN	
The least critical to buy organically are the Clean Fifteen list. The following are on the 2016 list:	
Avocados	Papayas
Corn	Kiw
Pineapples	Eggplant
Cabbage	Honeydew
Sweet peas	Grapefruit
Onions	Cantaloupe
Asparagus	Cauliflower
Mangos	

Some of the sweet corn sold in the United States are made from genetically engineered (GE) seedstock. Buy organic varieties of these crops to avoid GE produce.

Appendix 3 Index

GLADYS W. URIBE

Printed in Great Britain
by Amazon

16282469R00045